Goddess Enchantment
Magic and Spells

Volume 2: Goddesses of Love, Abundance and Transformation

Written and photographed
by Carrie Kirkpatrick

'Fortuna' written by
Markus Wolfson

Divine Media Ltd
London, United Kingdom
www.carriekirkpatrick.com

© 2011 Carrie Kirkpatrick

All worldwide rights reserved. No part of this book may be reproduced or utilized in any form or by any means, electronic or mechanical, including photocopying, recording, eBook formats, or by any information storage and retrieval system, without the express written permission from the publisher or author.

Cataloging-In-Publication Data
Goddess Enchantment Magic and Spells:
Volume 2: Goddesses of Love, Abundance and Tansformation
Kirkpatrick, Carrie
ISBN: 978-1-9160861-1-1
1.Non-Fiction 2. Religions 3. Pagan 4.Practices

Cover Art: Christine Moloney
To see more of Ms. Moloney's artwork please visit: www.myartisyours.co.uk
The picture of the Olympic Gold Medal on page 51 is used with the express written permission of the IOC.

Edition bound in the UK by IngramSpark
Electronic versions of this text are available. For more information visit: www.carriekirkpatrick.com
For eBook users, the images of the Goddesses in your eBook edition may be used in these rituals. Simply place your eReader on your altar with the image showing and complete the ritual outlined in the text.

Acknowledgements

Kleo Kay: Stylist, and for all her help and assistance.
Cover Art: Christine Moloney.
Researchers: Seldiy Bate, Gareth Medway and Maria Malo.
Graphic Design: Lewis Webb.
Photographic post production: Darren Richardson and Prapatson Richardson.
Additional photography: Kleo Kay, Alan Rider, Chris Robinson.
Shutterstock Photo Library.
The International Olympic Committee.
Brian Kannard.

Models: Anya Hastwell, Samantha Neal, Wendy Jane Paterson, Gemma Bowen, Liz Le Comber, Kleo Kay, Maria Antoniou, Christine Moloney and Louie Martin.

A special thanks to everyone in the community that donated their time, wisdom, and sage advice in the creation of this book.

All original photographs © Divine Media Ltd

Index

1	Chapter 1	Why Goddesses?
10	Chapter 2	Goddesses of Love
		Aphrodite
		Hathor
		Isis
40	Chapter 3	Goddesses of Success and Abundance
		Athena
		Nike
		Fortuna
68	Chapter 4	Goddesses of Transformation
		Hecate
		Arianrhod
		Ariadne

Why Goddesses?

Goddesses of Love, Abundance and Transformation' introduces the reader to a selection of Goddesses who are specifically associated with three main areas of spiritual and magical practice.

Goddesses from different pantheons are explored according to their areas of specialism, 'Love', 'Transformation', and 'Success and Abundance', and the reader can connect with them spiritually through visualisations and spells. This book presents both traditional and fresh new ways of connecting with the Goddesses and is intended as an introduction to the deities. Each Goddess is represented in a magical photograph, which can also serve as a focal point upon an altar.

The Goddesses are real, tangible and powerful energies that can be called upon to aid you, assist you and inspire you. Ultimately, Goddess magic works. Don't be afraid to ask for what you want, or more importantly for guidance and inspiration to know exactly what you want. The results will be rewarding and empowering.

There are many reasons why Goddesses are so popular in the modern spiritual world. For many, it is a case of redressing the balance after centuries of patriarchal religion and they feel drawn to rediscover the 'old ways', hearkening back to a time when there was not just one God, but a multitude of Gods and Goddesses that governed all aspects of life.

The Wiccan belief is that of a Goddess and a God who stand side by side, equal to each other. This concept is at the heart of this nature based religion, as the polarities of male and female are believed to be the key of life. Wicca's rapid growth in popularity within our modern world is a testament to the widespread appeal of this concept to those who see it as a more appropriate model for modern life.

For others, the route to the Goddess has come through self-development and their quest for personal empowerment. Their journey often calls upon them to question their upbringing and conditioning, and they may come to identify with a Divine Feminine principle, rather than the patriarchal divinities of mainstream religions. One way or another, ever since the Goddess movement took off during the middle of the Twentieth Century, women and men have been increasingly interested in exploring the concept of the Divine Feminine. Some people identify with only one Goddess, Mother Nature, the Earth. Others like to find the Goddess within themselves, to empower themselves and stand in their own power, maybe for the first time in their lives.

Priestesses tend to find their path to be a more devotional one, acknowledging individual Goddesses, seeking them out in the mythology of ancient times. Some Goddesses of the world are still very much alive within their cultures, whilst others have been long forgotten by their people and eagerly await their rediscovery.

Gatherings are frequently held of women and men celebrating the Goddess in ritual and song, awakening the Goddesses of many cultures and finding them alive and vibrant. If you are interested in exploring your spirituality then the Goddesses are a good place to start. Their energies are accessible and responsive, benevolent and kind.

Working magically with the Goddess energies is effective because, quite simply, it works. When referring to magical practice, it is the ability to influence one's external surroundings with one's mind that is meant, also known as projecting one's True Will. Others refer to this as Cosmic Ordering or The Law of Attraction.

The main point of any magical practice is to enhance your life, to be the best that you can be and to fulfil your true purpose in life, once you have discovered what that is. This is often referred to as finding your 'True Will', and is the meaning behind "Do what thou wilt shall be the whole of the Law" by Aleister Crowley. Knowing what you truly want is the key, and if in doubt, connect with one of the Goddesses and ask to know what it is that you truly want. Then, once you are clear about your intentions, there is nothing stopping you from attracting them towards you. You can confidently create a sacred space, call upon the deity, and ask for what you want, making sure you ask accurately for exactly what you want.

Working with the Goddess energies in magical practice adds power to the wishes and spells. Invoking the Goddesses also provides some extra guidance or insight into your own perceptions of your situation.

So if you then perform rituals which include the use of incenses, essential oils, mood enhancing music etc., then it is easy to achieve an altered state of consciousness quickly. Other factors can enhance the cosmic ordering process, the focussing of the will, such as performing the ritual at a particular moon phase, as the moon can act as an amplifier to your intentions. The inclusion of Goddesses in ritual practice is always beneficial, as they represent a higher energy

WHY GODDESSES?

source, a beneficial influence that can enhance a spell and guide the querent in a visualisation exercise.

Before commencing any of the exercises in this book, it is important to be aware of safety. When lighting candles, always ensure that they are placed safely away from anything that may catch fire. Make sure that the candles are secure in the candlestick, melting the bottom of the candle so that it sticks in the holder if necessary. The visualisations often require that you light a candle before closing your eyes and going into a meditative state, so please do be sensible.

When cleansing your space with salt and water, please take care not to sprinkle the water on anything electrical or surfaces that might be adversely affected by salt. A gentle sprinkling of the drops if water is sufficient, so please take care where you aim the water droplets.

When burning a sage smudge stick, always hold an ash tray beneath it as the embers can drop easily, running the risk of small burns. Please always ensure that the smudge stick is extinguished properly, this is sometimes difficult and may require running the smudge stick under the tap.

Creating a Sacred Space Short Version

Aim: To prepare the space for ritual work or visualisations with the Goddesses.
Tools: Rock salt, water, small bowl, incense, meditation music, white altar candle.

Cleanse the space as detailed above if necessary. If the energies do not need to be cleared, then simply sprinkle salt and water around the room and say: "With this salt and this water, I cleanse this space. May it be free from negativity, doubt and fear."

Light your incense and put on some soft meditation music. Light your altar candle. Close your eyes and visualise a halo of light around the candle flame. See it growing larger, growing as it expands until it becomes a golden ball of pulsating light. It becomes larger and larger, filling up the whole room. As it envelops the space you are at once free from all negativity, doubt and fear. It fills up the whole property and expands to the boundaries of the property. Now visualise the light from the candle flame coming towards you as a stream of light, and it illuminates your aura, making your energy bright and clear, vibrant and protected. You are safe within this sacred space. Now you can begin your ritual.

Creating a Sacred Space
Long Version including Chakra Balancing

Aim: To prepare the space for ritual work, to cleanse and revitalise the chakras before any ritual work or visualisations with the Goddesses.

Tools: Rock salt, water, small bowl, incense, meditation music, white altar candle.

Cleanse the space as detailed above if necessary. If the energies do not need to be cleared, then simply sprinkle salt and water around the room and say: "With this salt and this water, I cleanse this space. May it be free from negativity, doubt and fear."

    Light your incense and put on some soft meditation music. Light your altar candle. Close your eyes and visualise a halo of light around the candle flame. See it growing larger, growing as it expands until it becomes a golden ball of pulsating light. It becomes larger and larger, filling up the whole room. As it envelops the space you are at once free from all negativity, doubt and fear. It fills up the whole property and expands to the boundaries of the property. Visualise your base chakra, in the genital area, see it as a red ball of light. How does it appear to you? Is it dark red? Are there any dull patches on it? Visualise yourself picking up this red ball of light and tipping out any residue or dirt from it. Visualise it as thick tar, and as you tip it out, it goes into rich dark earth. Place the ball of light back at the base chakra and visualise a stream of light coming from the candle flame, charging up the red ball of light so that it shines a vibrant ruby red.

    Now move your attention to your sacral chakra, two inches below your belly button. See it as an orange ball of light. How does it appear to you? Is it dull, or dirty? Visualise yourself picking up the orange ball of light and tipping out any residue or dirt from it. See it as dark tar going into rich dark earth. Place the ball of light back at the sacral chakra and visualise a stream of light coming from the candle flame, charging up the orange ball of light until it glows with a vibrant orange light.

    Now move up to your solar plexus, your centre, in the centre of your rib cage. See this as a golden yellow ball of light. How does it look? Is it dull? Visualise yourself picking up the golden ball of light and tipping out any residue or dirt from it. See it as dark tar going into rich dark earth. Place the ball of light back at the solar plexus chakra and visualise a stream of light coming from the candle flame, charging up the golden ball of light until it glows with a vibrant yellow gold light.

WHY GODDESSES?

Now moving up to your heart chakra, in the centre of your chest, see a green ball of light. How does it look, is it dull? Visualise yourself picking up the green ball of light and tipping out any residue or dirt from it. See it as dark tar going into rich dark earth. Place the ball of light back at the heart chakra and visualise a stream of light coming from the candle flame, charging up the green ball of light until it glows with a vibrant emerald green light.

Moving up now to the throat chakra, in the centre of the throat, see this as a sky blue ball of light. How does it seem to you, is it bright blue or perhaps a little dull? Visualise yourself picking up the blue ball of light and tipping out any residue or dirt from it. See it as dark tar going into rich dark earth. Place the ball of light back at the throat chakra and visualise a stream of light coming from the candle flame, charging up the blue ball of light until it glows with a vibrant blue light.

Now take your attention to your third eye chakra, in the centre of your forehead. See this as an indigo ball of light. How does it seem to you? Visualise yourself picking up the indigo ball of light and tipping out any residue or dirt from it. See it as dark tar going into rich dark earth. Place the ball of light back at the third eye chakra and visualise a stream of light coming from the candle flame, charging up the indigo ball of light until it glows with a vibrant indigo light.

Now take your mind to your crown chakra, situated in the centre of the top of your head. See this as a violet ball of light. Visualise yourself picking up the violet ball of light and tipping out any residue or dirt from it. See it as dark tar going into rich dark earth. Place the ball of light back at the crown chakra and visualise a stream of light coming from the candle flame, charging up the violet ball of light until it glows with a vibrant purple light.

Your chakras are now cleared. You are safe and protected in your sacred space. Now you can begin your ritual.

LOVE GODDESSES
Aphrodite

Heavenly Goddess of Love and Beauty,
alluring lover of the night, we call to thee.
Beauteous *Goddess of Lovers*,
you are charming to the sight and are the source of all persuasion.
Secret Queen, you are both apparent and yet unseen,
the *most desired* by men and towards men inclined,
you are life giving, *beautiful* and kind.
Come, Cyprus born Goddess, and to my prayer incline,
exalted in the heavens where you shine, rejoicing in the azure shores,
near where the sea with foaming billows roars. *(i)*

Aphrodite is the Greek Goddess of Love and Beauty, of Sexuality and Desire. Her name means 'born of the sea foam'. According to legend, Gaia, the Goddess of Earth was married to Uranus, God of the Sky, but Gaia worried for their children's safety as Uranus hated them, fearing that they would depose him. She tried to protect her children from Uranus, but it became too difficult, so she arranged for one of her sons, Cronus, to castrate Uranus. This he did using a sickle made from flint, and as Uranus's testicles fell into the sea, they formed a great white foam where they landed. The flesh of Uranus was immortal, and out of the foam there emerged a beautiful and alluring Maiden Goddess, Aphrodite, also known as Venus in Rome, who rose fully formed from the sea. She floated on a scallop shell and was blown along the waves, by Zephyrus, the God of the Western Wind. This is depicted in the famous Botticelli painting of 'Venus'. She landed on the shore in

Cyprus and where she walked, flowers sprang up along the shores of the sea. Because of her seductive beauty, the Gods feared she would cause discord amongst them, and so Zeus married her off to Hephaestus, the God of Smithcraft, who was ugly and lame. Although he was not very attractive, Hephaestus was clever and a skilled craftsman. He made beautiful golden jewellery for the Goddess, which she adored, as she is enchanted by beautiful adornments. He also made her a magical girdle, which would make her even more irresistible to men.

Aphrodite loved material possessions, but what she really desired was passion. Hephaestus was a calm and mild mannered husband, but Aphrodite craved excitement and she was always seeking affairs. She embarked upon a passionate affair with the fiery God of War, Ares, also known as Mars in Rome. The affair continued for some time and they even had children, which Aphrodite pretended were her husband's. Helios, the Sun God saw what was going on and informed Hephaestus, who was heartbroken. Enraged, Hephaestus manufactured a bronze net, which was as fine as a spider's web, yet unbreakable, and he suspended it over his marriage bed. He then told Aphrodite that he was going away on a trip to Lemnos. His suspicions were confirmed when he returned the following morning to find Aphrodite and Ares entangled in his trap, and summoned all of the Gods to witness this dishonour. Later he relented and released them.

This episode did not stop Aphrodite from having more affairs. One affair was with Dionysus, the God of Wine, also known as Bacchus in Rome. She became pregnant again and she gave birth to a son called Priapus, who had an oversized erect penis. Statues of Priapus were placed in gardens in Ancient Greece to ward off bad luck. Another of Aphrodite's lovers was Adonis, who was eventually killed by a wild boar while hunting on Mount Lebanon. On the anniversary of his death, women would mourn him with much moaning and wailing. Adonis, whose name originates from Adonai, which means 'Lord', is a seasonal deity. In fact, the story was a Greek retelling of the Babylonian legend of Ishtar and her lover Tammuz, which was in turn a translation of the Sumerian legend of Inanna and Dumuzi. Aphrodite, Ishtar and Inanna were all Love Goddesses associated with the planet Venus, and were regarded by the ancients as the same deity, who merely had different names in different languages.

In the fourth century Aphrodite was separated into two aspects: higher, celestial love, Aphrodite Urania, and the love of the whole people, Aphrodite Pandemos, who is responsible for lower sexual life, and in particular for prostitution.

As Aphrodite came from the sea, she is the patroness of sailors and they pray to her for safe passage, to calm the waves and wind. She has the power to tame wild animals and is the bringer of peace.

Her sacred animals are fish, dolphins, doves, and swans. Her plants and scents are roses, apples, myrtle, lime trees, sandalwood. Her jewels are shells, pearls and gold. Also green gems like emerald or jade.

Working with Aphrodite can be very helpful for women who wish to be beautiful, seductive and empowered. Perhaps you have issues relating to low self-esteem, or think that you are not attractive enough to be deserving of love? Working magically with Aphrodite can help you to overcome those inhibitions, to restore your faith in your own attractiveness, to rediscover the lover within yourself, and have the confidence to love again, to flirt again and to have fun again.

Love Potion - Aphrodisia

Aim: To increase passion.
- 8 parts rose petals
- 3 parts rose geranium petals
- 1 part nutmeg
- 1 part lavender
- 1 part ginger
- 3 drops vanilla extract

Instructions
- Mix all of the ingredients and place in a tea pot.
- Add hot water and sweeten with honey to taste.
- Serve hot.

Aphrodite's Mirror Spell for Love

Aim: To heal and boost self-esteem and improve physical attractiveness.
Tools: Free standing mirror, pink candle, candlestick, rose oil.

Create a sacred space as detailed in Chapter One and dim the lights. Anoint the pink candle with rose oil and focus on the candle and say:

"Aphrodite, Goddess of Love and Beauty, I call to thee, that I may find you and you may find me within thy mirror, that I may rediscover my beauty again. As the beauty glows within, may I shine with beauty without and attract the right kind of love for me into my life, into my world, into my heart."

Light the candle and place it securely in the candlestick in front of the mirror. Now sit comfortably in front of the candle and mirror and gaze into the flickering flame and to the mirror beyond. Allow your eyes to soften their focus, even close them if you find it more comfortable, and start to visualise yourself in the mirror, happy, confident and relaxed. How do you look? See your vibrant energy shining back at you and see how attractive you are, see what it is that others like about you. Perhaps it is your smile, your warmth, your courage and your loyalty, perhaps it is also physical attributes that draw your attention. Now take time to look at your appearance, your hair, clothes and make up. See yourself adorning yourself, choosing clothes, dressing your hair, applying make up. What is it about your appearance that is different? What do you feel inspired to do that you don't already do?

A change is a good as a rest', and therefore a change in your physical appearance can be very beneficial when creating change in other areas of your life. Altering your physical appearance in some way will serve as a constant reminder every time you look in the mirror that you have entered a new chapter in your life, that you are a 'new version of you.' Take note of any details about your appearance and when you feel ready, bring your awareness back into your body. Refocus or open your eyes and write down any impressions that you received during the ritual. Let your candle burn all the way down.

Aphrodite Visualisation

Aim: To heal emotional hurts and boost confidence in romantic love relationships. To arouse sensuality and bring a new lover into your life, or to spice up an existing relationship.
Tools: Photo or statue of Aphrodite, pink and red candles, candlesticks (preferably a double candlestick), rose oil, cinnamon oil.
Incense: Jasmine.

Before starting this exercise it would be good to have a ritual bath.
Blend the following ingredients and add to your bath to induce lust and passion:

- 1 cup epsom salts
- $2/3$ cup sea salt
- $1/3$ cup baking soda
- 18 drops of rose oil
- 7 drops of jasmine oil
- 4 drops ylang ylang oil
- 7 drops neroli oil
- 3 drops rosemary oil
- Rose petals and rose geranium leaves and flowers.

After bathing, anoint yourself with scented body oil or lotion, preferably rose or jasmine, or blend your own oil, using a carrier oil as a base and adding the rose, jasmine, ylang ylang and neroli oils in the quantities detailed above. Dress yourself in something sensual, pretty lingerie, a soft flowing robe or diaphanous fabric. Now you are ready to begin. Prepare a sacred space as detailed in Chapter One. Light your altar candle and incense in front of your picture or statue of Aphrodite.

Call upon the Goddess Aphrodite, say: "Hail Aphrodite, Lady of Love and Delight, Who art throned amid the Cypress groves on the shore of the Great Sea." From the lamp in thy right hand pour shafts of light, pearly and emerald green. Thou art girdled with roses and emeralds, fire-opal and lapis lazuli. Thy voice is the music of doves, the breath of ecstasy.
Put forth the magic and mystery of thy beauty, to allure, to seduce, intoxicate and fascinate the soul. By the marriage of spirit and flesh, by the soft caress of the dove and the sharp caress of the serpent, I call upon thee, Aphrodite, to be here and bless me with your presence." (ii)

Take your pink candle and anoint it with rose oil for love, then take your red candle and anoint it with cinnamon oil for hot passion and say:

"As these two candles burn with their flames so bright, may the twin flames of passion between myself and my lover burn brightly with a fiery passion that enlivens us, a passion that endures and brings happiness to us both. Bestow upon us romantic love, sexual pleasure and desire, and bless our love that it may grow."

Now light your candles and place them next to each other in candlesticks (a twin candlestick would be best). Say: "So mote it be!"

Close your eyes and be aware of the two flames burning brightly before you. Allow your consciousness to go beyond the light of the flames and see yourself in a rocky landscape. You can hear the sea nearby, waves crashing on the beach, the rhythms of the tides. As you walk to the top of the rocks you see her reclining upon a day bed, swathed in delicate chiffon, surrounded by rose petals. Behold Aphrodite, a most beautiful Goddess with long flowing locks of golden hair, radiant beauty and sensuality. She fixes her gaze upon you, and you gaze into the depths of her captivating blue eyes. To her left a beautiful white dove stretches its wings and coos softly. She reaches out her hand and takes yours, standing up she holds you in her warm embrace, then she leads you by the hand down a path set in the rock face, down towards the sea. As you both reach the soft sandy beach she invites you to remove your shoes and enter the water. At first you just venture a little way, allowing the water to wash over your toes, feeling its fresh chill but soon becoming accustomed to its touch. Aphrodite tells you that it's time to embrace the waves, surrender to passion and emotion. And she leads you further into the sea, laughing and splashing and dancing with the waves. As you go forth you are pleasantly surprised to find that the water is not too cold, instead it stimulates you, invigorates you, and before long you are being swept this way and that by the current and the waves. Say aloud the past emotional hurts that you wish to let go of, and ask for new love to come into your life. Invite sensuality and beauty into your world, to be able to indulge your fantasies and embrace your passions.

How do you feel? Are you afraid of losing yourself to the sea? Can you touch the seabed or are you now floating with the current, feeling the rhythm of the waves, back and forth, back and forth? After a while you find yourself once again at the seashore with the beautiful Goddess Aphrodite beside you, giggling and breathless, her white chiffon robe dishevelled and wet, clinging to her breasts and revealing her beauty. Ask Aphrodite for your heart's desire and any advice she may have to offer you to help you to achieve it. Perhaps lessons in flirtation, sexual confidence, to feel pretty and to make the most of one's appearance?

LOVE GODDESSES

> *Exquisitely enthroned*, immortal Aphrodite,
> weaver of charms, I beg you, *Golden Lady*,
> do not crush my heart with sickness and distress.
> *Beautiful birds* drew you swiftly from heaven over the black earth
> through the air between with the rapid flutter of their downy wings.
> Swiftly they came and you, O blessed Goddess, smiling in your *immortal beauty*
> asked what I wished for most in my frenzied heart. Come to me now, free me from my
> harsh anxieties; and grant that which *my heart longs for*. (iii)

Aphrodite removes the golden girdle from around her waist and offers it to you, you put it on and feel her confidence, pretty and flirtatious, joyful in the knowledge that romantic and passionate love is yours for the sharing. As the water skims your feet and your toes, she reveals a secret to you, imparting some of her knowledge of the art of love and desire. When you are ready, you both leave the seashore and ascend once again the rocky cliff until you reach the top, where Aphrodite embraces you and reminds you that you may return to her at any time. You thank her and bid her farewell, and make your way back down the rocks towards two bright lights that glow before you. As you draw closer they shine ever more brightly and you find yourself passing through the light, the light which you recognise now as the twin flames of your red and pink candles. See yourself sitting or lying in your meditation and re-enter your body. Bring your awareness back to your toes, wiggling them and become conscious of your breathing. In your own time, open your eyes.

Thank Aphrodite for her presence and say: "Aphrodite, I thank you for your presence here today, and I bid you, hail and farewell!"

Let your candles burn down safely overnight.

LOVE GODDESSES

Hathor

We exalt you to the height of *heaven*.
Great Goddess of *Love and Beauty*,
Bestow your gifts upon us,
That we may *embrace love* with a joyous heart.
You are the Mistress of Music, the *Lady of the Dance*,
We praise your Majesty every day,
From dusk until the Earth grows light,
We praise you with song. We dance for your Majesty
And *your heart rejoices* over our performance. *(iv)*

Hathor is the Egyptian Goddess of Love, Beauty, Music and Dance and well as Drunkenness, Joy and Motherhood. She was one of the most important and popular deities throughout the history of Ancient Egypt. She was also a fertility Goddess who helped women in childbirth. Hathor is often depicted as a woman with a cow's head, or a woman's head with cow horns, and she often has a sun disc set in between the horns. She has cow ears and a simple hair style, parted in the middle. She wears a special necklace, the Menat, which is used as a musical instrument and she also carries the sistrum, an instrument which sounds similar to a tambourine. Music is a source of great joy to Hathor and it is a good way to call her to you.

As the Goddess of Love and Beauty, Hathor is very sensuous and will use her femininity for the good of the people. According to myth, when Ra, the Sun God, was upset and hid himself away, she did a strip tease in front of him, which cheered him up and made the Sun shine again. This story was probably used to explain a solar eclipse.

Hathor's name means 'House of Horus', which indicates a connection between the Goddess and the sky particularly, the Milky Way, which was seen by the Ancient Egyptians as milk that flowed from the Celestial Cow. The Milky Way was also known as the 'Nile of the Sky'. It was believed that the annual flooding of the river Nile in Egypt, which was of vital importance to the fertility of the land, was Hathor's responsibility.

Hathor was also responsible for the breaking of the waters before childbirth. Pregnant women would call upon Hathor for protection during childbirth, and also ask her to predict the future of their newborn babies. Newborn children are believed to be visited by seven Hathors, who would determine their fate. Due to her connections with childbirth, Hathor also became known as the guardian of midwives and was worshipped by women during childbirth as well as young girls seeking a husband.

Hathor is among the most ancient of the Egyptian deities and features prominently in the creation story with Ra, the Sun God. Hathor remained an important deity in Egyptian culture for as long as worship of the traditional Egyptian Gods was permitted. In modern times, Hathor continues to be popular with Westerners who seek spiritual inspiration in Ancient Egyptian mysticism and she is still honoured, discreetly, by local Egyptian women who ask for healing, fertility and protection at the remains of her shrines.

Hathor was the Goddess of all things that were considered to be the pleasures of life 5,000 years ago. In many cases, these are still regarded as the pleasures of life today: joy, love, romance, abundance, dance, music, alcohol and perfume. She was primarily a deity of women and she ruled everything to do with being a woman.

However, she was also worshipped by the miners in the Sinai Peninsula, who would ask for her blessing and protection as they dug deep into the Earth. The gemstones associated with Hathor are turquoise, lapis lazuli and malachite, which were mined in that area. Malachite would be ground up into a fine powder and used to make black eye make up. As Malachite is one of Hathor's gemstones, it was seen as a fitting act of devotion to wear what was seen as her 'essence' around one's eyes.

Hathor embodies all abundance in life, whether it be an abundance of beauty, joy, wealth and security. She is the embodiment of success and has a steely focus that will not let her deter from her goals. Working with Hathor can help you to heal your self-esteem, bring back laughter and joy, love and beauty into your life. She can help you to attract a new lover into your life, or help you as you move into motherhood. Hathor can also help you to appreciate your true worth

LOVE GODDESSES

as a woman, to become and feel beautiful and elegant all the time. Ask her to bestow her gifts of joy upon you in your mundane world and walk with her beauty every day.

Hathor's Mirror Spell

Aim: To attract love into your life.
Tools: Pink or red candle, candlestick, rose or jasmine oil, handheld mirror. Egyptian / inspiring music.
Incense: Jasmine.

Create a sacred space as detailed in Chapter One. Light the incense, turn down the lights so that they are very low, and play the music softly. Anoint the candle with rose or jasmine oil and as you focus on the candle, call upon the Goddess, say:

"Great Goddess Hathor, Goddess of Love, of Beauty and Joy, I ask that you be here present this night, that I may voice my true desire for a lover in my life who will lift my heart with passionate joy. May they be guided to my side that we may share a love so true. May our hearts sing with joy in honour of you. Guide me to be in the right place at the right time to meet my heart's desire, and that they be ready and willing to love me with a passion equal to mine. Show me my new love, O Goddess divine."

Now light the candle and place it in the candlestick on a table and say: "So mote it be!" Take the handheld mirror and gaze into it, illuminated only by the light of the candle. Allow your eyes to lose their focus and as you look at your reflection in the low flickering light, see if another face appears before you. Who is it? Is it someone you already know? Perhaps you will see yourself in a particular situation, look at where you are, taking note of the details. How do you appear? Who else is there? This may be where you meet your lover. When you feel ready, re-focus your eyes and bring your awareness back into the room. Thank Hathor for giving you the vision to see your new love and say: "Hail and farewell!" Let your candle burn all the way down.

Spell to Attract New Love into Your Life

Aim: To boost self-esteem and increase your confidence in love relationships; to help bring about personal transformation; to attract love into your life; to become more flirtatious and develop social skills.

Tools: Statue or picture of Hathor, tea light candle to place in front of the Goddess, tea light holder, pink candle, orange candle, candle sticks, rose quartz, rose oil, bergamot oil, citrine, and rose petals.

Offerings: Chocolate, sweet wine, and some beautiful flowers

Prepare a sacred space as detailed in Chapter One. Place your tools on a table in front of you in a darkened room. Light the tea light candle and place it in front of the photo or statue. Scatter the rose petals upon the altar. Call upon the beautiful Goddess Hathor, Goddess of Love, Goddess of Beauty, Goddess of Dance and Joy and say:

"I call upon Hathor, great Goddess of Egypt, Queen of the Dance, I ask you be present here tonight, Great Goddess of Love, who heals the heart. Goddess of Joy and Self-esteem, bless me with your presence so that I may be inspired by your magic and grant my wishes. Great Goddess Hathor, I bid you, hail and welcome!"

Look upon your picture or statue and make an offering to the Goddess, perhaps some sweet wine, some chocolate, a beautiful flower – or all three. As you do so, say:

"Beautiful Hathor, Goddess of Love and Beauty, please accept these offerings and grant me your guidance and your blessings. So mote it be!"

Take your pink candle and anoint it with rose oil. Hold it in front of you as you stand before the Goddess. Ask aloud for your wish, be clear and concise in your language, and pay attention to detail. For example, if it is a new relationship that you seek, ask:

"I wish to be one half of a loving, happy relationship, which is exactly the right kind of love for me, when the time is right."

Holding the rose quartz, visualise yourself happily enjoying the experience of your wish. A good way to do this is to imagine a TV set, you are watching a film and you are the central character. See yourself smiling happily and looking back out at yourself. See the details in the picture, you are at home, perhaps there are children in this scene, perhaps evidence of your work which you love. All of the ingredients of your everyday life can be in this picture, but the most important thing is to see yourself smiling happily and full of energy, thriving on the combination of everything in your life, able to take everything in your stride. Then you see your lover in the picture, you feel a warmth in your heart as you know that you are loved, and that you are in love. You cannot see their face, for they are turned the other way, probably doing something useful like fixing you a drink or cooking supper! But the most important thing to focus on is yourself enjoying the end result of your desires. Open your eyes and light your candle from the altar candle and say aloud: "So mote it be!" Light the candle and place it on the altar next to your rose quartz. Take your orange candle and anoint it with bergamot oil. Ask Hathor for the confidence and courage to speak up, to interact, to flirt, to dance. If you are sometimes shy around new people and potential lovers, then ask her that you may overcome your shyness and be filled with the joy of interacting with others, the confidence to relax and laugh, the energy to communicate and have fun. Holding the citrine, close your eyes, and visualise yourself having fun, flirtatious and confident, interacting with others with confidence and joy. Open your eyes and light your candle, say: "So mote it be!". Safely and securely put the candle in the candlestick and place the citrine next to it. Focus on your statue or picture of Hathor and summarise once again that which you desire. Close your eyes and see her in your mind's eye. Perhaps she will speak to you or dance with you. What does she say, how do you feel? Take note of any feelings or images that arise in your mind and when you feel ready, open your eyes.
Thank Hathor for blessing you with her presence and listening to your wishes, and say:

"Until the next time, I bid you, hail and farewell!"

Then leave your candle in a safe place to burn all the way down.

Magic Mirror of Transformation Spell

Aim: To heal the heart of past emotional hurts, to boost confidence and self-esteem, to bring about personal transformation and boost one's self image.

Tools: A mirror, pink candle, orange candle, candlesticks, rose quartz crystal, tea light candle, rose or jasmine oil, and grapefruit or bergamot oil.

Prepare a sacred space as detailed in Chapter One. In a darkened room, set your mirror on the table in front of you and light a tea light and place it near by so that you can sit comfortably and gaze into it. Call upon the Goddess Hathor to be with you, to guide you and to bestow her blessings upon you. Call her name three times, you can chant it if you prefer as the sound vibration of singing her name can be very uplifting, chant: "Hathor, Hathor, Hathor!" Take your pink candle and anoint it with rose or jasmine oil, to resonate with the heart chakra. Ask that you may find love within yourself, that your heart be healed so that you may love yourself and love with another. Tell Hathor about the emotional pain you have endured, how it happened, and how you feel. Then ask her to heal that hurt, release that pain, so that it no longer restricts you. Ask for her guidance as to what you need to change about yourself in order to bring the confidence and love into your life that you desire. As you conclude your wish say: "So mote it be!" and light your candle from the tea light, and place it in the candlestick. Now take your orange candle and anoint it with bergamot or grapefruit oil, to induce energy, enthusiasm, optimism. Ask for the confidence and energy to follow through with your personal transformation, to move forward into your own happier future, to have the motivation to express yourself happily and joyfully. Then light your candle and say: "So mote it be!" Set the candle in the candlestick safely and securely. Place the two candles one either side of your mirror and gaze into the mirror. Allow your eyes to defocus a little, perhaps they might feel a little watery, if so that is fine. See what impressions form in the reflection, perhaps you see your face change, your hair, your demeanour, your clothes. What colours are you wearing? Look at your image and ask yourself:

"What do I need to do to become who I want to be? What shall I do first?"

Take note of the answers that come into your mind. When you are ready re-focus your eyes and write down the impressions that you received. Thank the Goddess Hathor for her guidance and inspiration and go ahead with the suggestions that you picked up during the ritual. Let your candles burn all the way down.

Hathor Visualisation

Aim: To heal the heart and to restore self-esteem and confidence. To re-awaken the pretty woman within oneself.

Tools: Photo or statue of Hathor, pink candle, rose oil, rose quartz crystal, jasmine incense.

Create a sacred space as detailed in Chapter One. Light your incense and place it before the photo or statue of Hathor. Call upon the Goddess, say:

"Great Goddess Hathor, I call to thee, that you may be here now with me, bestow your magic, my heart to heal and may joyful love be mine to feel."

Sit or lie in a comfortable position and place a lit pink candle in front of you, which you have anointed with rose oil. Place a piece of rose quartz crystal on your heart chakra or hold it in your hand. Focus on the candle and see a halo of golden light surrounding the flame. Close your eyes and visualise this golden halo of light as it starts to grow, expanding into a sphere of golden light. This ball of light continues to grow, becoming bigger and bigger until you are completely enveloped in its radiant light. All at once you feel yourself free from negativity, doubt and fear – bathed in this beautiful golden pulsating light. The sphere of light continues to grow until it fills the room, the building, extending to the boundaries of the building. You bask in the warm glow of this golden light, feeling its gentle warmth and you realise that this is your sacred space, where you can be safe and secure within this protective bubble, free from negativity, doubt and fear. Focus once again upon the flickering flame of your pink candle, and see the energy of the flame come towards you and envelop you in white light, starting at your base chakra, and rising through all of your chakras until it reaches your crown chakra at the top of your head. The light flows over your head and down your back and then up through the chakras again, a circular current of white golden light, cleansing and energising your chakras, revitalising your energy, releasing you from the psychic and energetic connections that surround us every day. In your mind or spoken out loud affirm:

"I hereby cut all ties with everyone, just for the purposes of this meditation, safe in the knowledge that all positive ties will be reformed afterwards."

This frees you from all of your connections with others, just for the duration of this visualisation.

Visualise yourself in front of a golden rose arch, with beautiful wild roses entwined all around it and a gossamer veil hanging across it, fluttering gently in the breeze. In your mind's eye, see yourself get up and walk towards the rose arch. Pull aside the gossamer veil and walk through. You are now entering a magical garden, with wild flowers and rose bushes all around. You walk along a path, and the rose bushes become taller and more rambling until they meet above your head, blocking out the light with their branches entwined above you. The tunnel they form becomes a little darker until you need to stoop your head a little. You realise that you have entered into the side of a hill and are in a tunnel, but you carry on towards a rosy, golden light that you can see ahead of you. After a while the tunnel opens up and you find yourself within a beautiful cavern made of natural rose quartz crystal, whose walls are aglow with a soft pink and gold light which appears to emanate from deep within the rock. Touch the walls of crystal and feel the healing energy flooding into your hands, for this is a healing cavern where you can return at any time to heal your heart. The warmth from the rock moves along your arms and instantly fills you with strength and energy, centring on your heart chakra, where the soft pink light from the crystal cleanses and revitalises your heart centre. Close your eyes for a moment or two and see your heart chakra start to glow with a beautiful emerald green light.

On the other side of the cavern you see her for the first time, her swirling skirts of green and gold fluttering and shimmying as the she dances towards you, spinning around, tossing her beautiful flowing locks. Behold Hathor, Egyptian Goddess of Love and Beauty and Goddess of the Dance. She stops before you and you bask in her radiant beauty, with delicate jewels upon her face and in her hair, her skin glistens with vibrant energy. Ask her that which you wish to know or what it is you wish for. Perhaps she will give you a gift or simply hold you in her warm, sensuous embrace. This is the Goddess who will heal your heart, restore your self-esteem, make you feel pretty again, rediscover the lover within yourself, and bring joy back once again into your world.

Hathor takes you over to a dark pool of water at the side of the cavern, where you can gaze upon the reflection of the two of you as you look into its dark depths. Hathor skims her hand across the water and the image dissolves into a cascade of ripples. As the water stills itself, a new image forms, this time it has changed, with the magical touch of the Goddess. As the image becomes clear you see yourself - happy, smiling and filled with love and joy. Pay attention to the details of your reflection - how are you dressed? Look at your hair, make-up, jewellery. Where are you? This image represents the future you, healed of heart and full of joy. See this, feel this and believe that this is now a part of you. After a while you stand up and thank the Goddess Hathor for her magical gifts and healing. You take your leave of the Goddess, safe in the knowledge that you may return to see her at any time. She will always be here for you in her healing cave - your sanctuary.

You enter once again into the tunnel that leads from the rose quartz cavern, and out into the overgrown wild and magical garden. As you proceed on your way, the sun starts to break through the overgrown branches above your head, the rose bushes become smaller and you find yourself once again in front of the rose arch with the gossamer veil fluttering in the gentle breeze. You pull the veil to one side and step through and find yourself back in your room. You can see yourself sitting or lying in front of the pink candle, holding your rose quartz crystal. Walk over to your body and step back in. Gently bring your awareness back into your body, wiggle your toes, become aware of your breathing and in your own time, open your eyes. Make sure that your candle is securely fixed in the candleholder and leave it to burn all the way down.

Make a note of what you saw when you gazed into the scrying pool and consider implementing any changes to your physical appearance that were revealed to you.

LOVE GODDESSES

Isis

I am Isis, mistress of every land, I decreed laws for humanity,
and ordained things that cannot be changed.
I am the wife and sister of *King Osiris*,
I am she who governs Sirius the Dog Star,
I am she who is called *divine amongst women*,
I divided the earth from the heavens, I manifested the paths of the stars,
I prescribed the courses of the *sun and the moon*,
I made Justice mighty, I brought women and men together,
I revealed *initiations* to humanity, I founded sanctuaries of the Gods,
I compelled men to love women. (v)

Isis is the Egyptian Goddess of Love, Motherhood, Fertility and Magic. Her name was originally Aset, which means 'throne', however when she was adopted by the Romans and Greeks, they renamed her as 'Isis' and it is this name that remained. As her name meant 'The Lady of the Throne', this implied that the pharaoh owed his position to her. She is depicted as having dark hair and often wears a throne as a crown. She is also shown holding a lotus in her hand. Her symbols are the Ankh and Isis Knot. The Ankh is a well-known symbol, representing Eternal Life and it is believed that the Isis Knot, which is a hieroglyphic symbol, represents the blood from Isis' womb and therefore this symbol reaffirms Isis' connection with fertility and women's magic. She was also commonly portrayed with a ritual bucket used for holy Nile water, and a sistrum, a kind of rattle used in her worship. Other representations show Isis suckling her son, Horus. She is sometimes depicted as wearing a head dress with the solar disk between two cow horns, which is the same as the head dress worn by Hathor. According to her myth, Isis is one of the children of Nuit, the Sky Goddess, and Geb, the Earth God. She married her brother, Osiris, the God of Vegetation and of Resurrection. Osiris and Isis were bringers of civilisation to Egypt. Isis brought humanity gifts of wheat and corn, and taught her people the arts of agriculture. She also taught them how to brew beer.

    As Osiris was the God of Vegetation, he was closely linked to the cycle of life. His myth tells of his death and resurrection which parallels the death and rebirth of vegetation during the course of the year. Osiris' brother, the God Set, the Destroyer, was very jealous and plotted to kill him. At a festival he persuaded Osiris to get into a coffin, apparently as a joke. However, as soon as Osiris complied, Set locked him in the coffin, and threw it into the river Nile. Isis was distraught when she heard the terrible news and immediately cut off her hair and wore the robes of mourning. Stricken with grief, she searched the whole of Egypt, looking for her beloved husband. She eventually recovered the coffin, but not Osiris' body. Set had found the body first and had hacked it into fourteen parts and then scattered them across the land. Isis sought the help of her sister, Nephthys, and together they recovered all the pieces of her husband's body, except one, the phallus, which had been eaten by a fish. Isis made another phallus out of gold and with her magic, she brought Osiris back to life. Osiris then became associated with life after death. Isis and Osiris then conceived a son, Horus, after his resurrection.

    Another legend of Isis is told in the Turin Papyrus. Isis knew that the Sun God, Ra, had a secret name, which bestowed great power, and she was determined to find out what it was so as to gain more power. She devised a plan and created a serpent out of earth and saliva, which she placed in the path of Ra, and she waited. Everything went as she wished and the serpent bit Ra. Its poison spread 'swiftly through his flesh just as the Nile rushes through all of his land.' The other Gods of Egypt tried to help Ra, but they were unable to cure him. Then Isis spoke to Ra, and said that she would cure him but only if he would tell her his secret name. At first he refused, then eventually he told her: "I am Khepera in the morning, I am Ra at noon and I am Temu at evening." But Isis knew that none of these were his secret name, and so she withheld her cure. Finally, Ra was in so much pain, he gave in. There followed a period of darkness on the Earth, during which Ra told Isis his secret name and Isis then cured him, saying: "Depart thou poison, go forth from Ra, let Ra live. These are the words of Isis, mighty lady, mistress of Gods, who knows Ra by his own name." This story was probably told to explain a total eclipse of the sun. However, the papyrus omits to reveal the secret name of Ra to us mere mortals.

    Isis was such an all-encompassing Goddess, that the Greeks were uncertain how to relate her to their own pantheon. The historian Herodotus identified her with Demeter, the Corn Goddess, but others thought that she was Aphrodite, Goddess of Love. In the Latin novel Metamorphoses (also known as The Golden Ass) by Apuleius, the unhappy hero, Lucius, who had dabbled in magic as a young man and got into trouble, finally prayed to the Goddess Isis,

LOVE GODDESSES

33

whom he regarded as a universal deity:

"Queen of Heaven, whether thou art the kindly Ceres, the mother from whom sprang the fruits of the earth, who, joyous at the discovery of thy daughter, didst banish the savage nutriment of the ancient acorn, and pointing out sweeter food, who dost now till the soil of Eleusis; or whether thou art celestial Venus, who, in the first origin of things, didst associate the different sexes, through the creation of mutual love, and having propagated an eternal offspring in the human race, art now worshipped in the sea-girt shrine of Paphos; or whether thou art [Diana] the sister of Phoebus, who, by relieving the pangs of women in travail by soothing remedies, hast brought into the world multitudes so innumerable, and art now venerated in the far-famed shrines of Ephesus; or whether thou art Proserpine, terrific with midnight howlings, whose three-fold visage checks the attack of the ghosts, closing the recesses of the earth, and who wandering over many a grove, art propitiated by various modes of worship with that feminine brightness of thine, illuminating the walls of every city, and with thy vaporous beams nurturing the joyous seeds of plants, and for the revolutions of the sun ministering thy fitful gleams; by whatever name, by whatever ceremonies, and under whatever form it is lawful to invoke thee; do thou graciously succour me in this my extreme

LOVE GODDESSES

> I am *all* that was, and *all* that is, and *all* that ever shall be,
> and no mortal man has ever *raised my veil*. (vi)

distress, support my fallen fortune, and grant me rest and peace, after the endurance of so many sad calamities. Let there be an end of my sufferings, let there be an end of my perils."

After this he fell asleep, and was promptly rewarded with a vision of the Goddess herself, garlanded with flowers, her hair in luxurious ringlets, her robe many-coloured, her mantle of the deepest black, her fragrance as the perfumes of Arabia, who spoke directly to him:
"Behold me, Lucius; moved by thy prayers, I appear to thee; I, who am Nature's mother, the mistress of all the elements, the primordial offspring of time, the supreme among deities, the Queen of departed spirits, the first of the celestials, and the uniform manifestation of the Gods and Goddesses; who govern by my rod the luminous heights of heaven, the salubrious breezes of the ocean, and the anguished silent realms of the shades below: whose one solid divinity the whole orb of the earth venerates under a manifold form, with different rites, and under a variety of appellations."

Isis is seen as the protective Mother-Goddess, often depicted with golden wings. She became a guide to the Underworld and as Lady of Magic and Medicine, who has power over life and death. Isis taught women how to handle their men-folk, and she would be invoked by women who needed love or domestic harmony. She is also champion of poor or weak people, the homeless, orphans and the underprivileged.
Her flowers are the lotus and the rose, her plants and perfumes are cedar, heather and tamarisk. Her animals are the cow, the hawk and the kite. Her gems are the carnelian and lapis lazuli.

Many are drawn to work with Isis more than any other Goddess, and she is the most famous Goddess of world history. She provides inspiration in many different areas: from the fierce and loyal love she felt for her husband; to the mother's love for her son; the love of a Queen for her people; protectress of women in childbirth and Mistress of Magic.

You can work with Isis if you need help and guidance in any of the aforementioned areas: perhaps you would like to develop your psychic abilities, intuition and magical skills; or perhaps you would like help with your relationships, either with your lover or your child. Perhaps you need help in supporting the family unit. Whatever it is that you seek, you will surely find the answer with Isis. She is often represented with her wings outstretched, and working with Isis can

empower you to spread your own wings so that you may soar to new heights personally and in your life, or wrap her protective wings around you if you feel vulnerable.

Sacred Waters of Isis Spell

Aim: To enhance your intuition and abilities of clairvoyance. To be able to use your intuition to choose a suitable lover.

Tools: Photo or statue of Isis, tea light candle and holder, pink candle for enduring love and silver candle for psychic development, candlesticks, sandalwood incense, dark bowl of water, soft meditative music, paper and pen.

Create a sacred space as detailed in Chapter One. Play the music, not too loudly. Light the tea light candle and place it in front of the image of Isis. Light the incense and call upon the Goddess, say:

> "Great Isis of the Sacred Veil,
> I call to thee to teach me well,
> that I may know the path ahead
> and by my inner sight be led.
> Develop psychic gifts of sight
> to see beyond, to know what's right.
> All this I ask to share with thee,
> Great Isis, Goddess, be with me."

Light the pink candle and ask for true love in your life in all relationships. Light the silver candle and ask for clear sight (clairvoyance), good intuition and psychic abilities. Place one candle either side of the bowl of water, in front of the image of Isis. Start to scry in the water, allow your eyes to lose their focus and gaze into the water. Allow images to form in your mind, perhaps your mind will wander and you will find yourself thinking of a situation or a person. Allow this to unfold and go where it takes you. When you feel ready, bring your attention back to yourself and allow your eyes to refocus. Take a few deep breaths and write down any impressions that you had, what did you see, feel or hear?

When you are ready, thank the Goddess for her presence and her gifts to you and bid her:

"Hail and farewell!" Let your candles burn all the way down. Take note of any dreams that you have over the next few days.

Visualisation for Isis

Aim: To connect with Isis and to spread your wings to develop confidence.
Tools: White or silver candle, sandlewood incense

Create a sacred space as detailed in Chapter One. Light a white or silver candle, light the incense sit or lie in front of it and close your eyes. Be aware of the candle burning brightly, focus your inner vision on the flame, and let your awareness take you beyond the flickering light. You are surrounded by a golden pulsating light, and you can feel its warmth embracing and energising you. As you look up and around you, you find yourself on a desert plain, feel the rich warm sand beneath your feet, and feel the heat of the sun shining brightly overhead. The sky is a piercing radiant blue as you have never seen before. The sun is sitting low in the sky, just above the horizon, and you walk towards its beautiful bright light. As you come closer towards the intense and powerful light, you sense a movement from within, a fluttering, and as you draw closer, you can make out a figure, a beautiful Goddess dressed in white and adorned with Lapis and Gold. She raises her arms up to the sun, and you now see the Wings of Isis unfold before you revealing a majestic, all powerful Goddess, radiant, resplendent, and shining with the light of Ra, the Sun God. As she stands before you, you feel her strength and her power. Feel her radiance, feel yourself nourished by her energy. She nods to you and asks you to step forward. Do not fear her power as this is Isis, Goddess of Love, Mystery and Magic.

As you step closer, she smiles and then welcomes you into her embrace, wrapping her beautiful vibrant lapis blue and gold wings around you. She asks you, what do you seek, what is your desire – be it knowledge of the higher planes or more earthly matters. Stay in her embrace for as long as you wish, feel her protection, her healing warmth and her inspiration. Be rejuvenated by her light.

When she lowers her wings, you see before you a beautiful landscape and realise that you are standing on top of a sand dune. Ahead of you, flying through the deep blue sky, you see a bird, soaring and swooping, calling to you.

Take note of what kind of bird this is, and how do you feel? For this bird represents you. You, as you spread your wings and fly. This bird will teach you who you are and how to proceed with your current situation into your beautiful future. The bird swoops down and flies past you, perhaps it lands upon your arm. As it does, you feel at one with your future self and Isis speaks to you. Listen to your message and understand the power of Isis - protectress, mother, lover,

LOVE GODDESSES

wife, Queen, Goddess, sorceress, seer. She is here to help you, to guide and inspire you. She has imparted a little of that power to you today, and as you follow your journey you will always feel her with you, all you have to do is just call her name: "Hail Isis, Hail Isis, Hail Isis!"

When you are ready, your bird flies off once again and circles above you. You thank Isis for her help and turn back from whence you came, safe in the knowledge that you may revisit her at any time. Walking back across the warm, golden sand dunes, you once again find yourself bathed in the warmth and light of the sun. Brighter and brighter it shines, until you are completely enveloped in its golden light. As you continue forward, the light starts to soften and fade, and you find yourself once again back in your room, in front of your candle. See yourself sitting or lying, and bring your consciousness back into your body. Take a few deep breaths and when you are ready open your eyes.

Write down everything that Isis told you. Which bird did you see? Refer to this over the coming days and weeks and watch how your situation unfolds.

In the beginning there was Isis: Oldest of the Old,
She was the Goddess from whom all Becoming of the House of Life,
Mistress of the ***Word of God.*** She was the unique.
In all her great and wonderful works she was a ***wiser magician***
and more excellent than any other God. *(vii)*

SUCCESS AND ABUNDANCE
Athena

Hail Athena, Goddess of Wisdom and Will, Thou art throned in the noble city
Where men and women dare to speak freely.
Thou art the Virgin *Mother of liberty*.
Let thy sword be ever ready, Lady of resolute courage,
And let the Lamp of thy *wisdom shine* forth
That *True Will* may be illumined and guided by reason.
Wherever there is the will to stand against tyranny,
Wherever war gives way to reason,
Wherever peace is founded on courage and wisdom,
We have seen the glint of thy sword.
By the *mysterious owl*, wise bird of night,
By graceful olive, tree of patience and peace,
By the sharp pointed lance, symbol of True Will
I call to you great Goddess, to be with us. [i]

The ancient origins of this magnificent Goddess herald her as the Goddess of Women. In Minoan Crete she was primarily a household Goddess who governed all domestic crafts, especially dressmaking and weaving. As time passed and patriarchy took over, she was adopted as the patron of Athens and started to assume more masculine attributes. She became known as Goddess of War, of Justice, of Success and Victory, and is often depicted with a spear or sword, helmet

and shield. Although she is a Goddess of War, she is seen more as a Goddess who would always seek a peaceful resolution first, before resorting to aggression. However, once engaged in combat she always wins and is often represented as holding the Goddess of Success and Victory, Nike, in her hand.

According to myth, the God Zeus lusted after Metis, who tried to avoid his attentions. In her attempts to escape him, she transformed herself into many different shapes, until at last he caught her and made her pregnant. An oracle of Mother Earth predicted that Metis would give birth to a daughter, and that if she went on to have another child, it would be a boy. This boy would grow up and depose Zeus, in the same way that Zeus had deposed his father, Cronus, and Cronus had deposed his own father Uranus before him. Zeus was so alarmed by this prophecy, that he wanted to take steps to prevent it, so he lured Metis to come and rest on his couch. He then used his magic to make her very small and swallowed her. He later claimed that she was giving him advice from within his belly. Months passed by, and one day Zeus was struck by a severe headache as he walked along the shores of Lake Triton. The pain in his head was excruciating and he thought that his head would burst. As he screamed with pain, his cries were heard for miles around and the Gods Hermes and

SUCCESS AND ABUNDANCE

Hephaestus came to his aid. Hephaestus cracked open Zeus's skull with a blow from his axe, and Athena leapt fully formed from Zeus's head, uttering a warlike cry. As she was born via a form of caesarean birth from his head, and her mother Metis was also a guardian of the power of the planet Mercury, Athena became associated with rational thinking and strategy.

Athena was known as a Virgin Goddess, which does not necessarily refer to her lack of sexual experience, but rather to the fact that she was never affiliated to a God. Her domain was always hers and hers alone, and therefore she represents independent women, who are not 'owned' by a husband or father. She presided over Athens, and her temple, the Parthenon (which is derived from the word parthenos, meaning virgin), became known as the centre for wisdom in the whole of the Hellenic world.

Her totem animals are the owl, which sits upon her shoulder, representing wisdom, and the snake, representing the power of transformation, which is usually shown upon her shield.

Working with Athena can help you if you wish to enhance your motivation and persistence and if you require help in achieving your goals. She helps women to achieve independence and stand up for

themselves. You can ask Athena to help you to obtain justice in a given situation, and to devise a good strategy when facing challenging situations or opposition. When the situation requires that you have a level head and not be ruled by your emotions, Athena is the Goddess to call upon that will help you to win. She is very helpful in all matters of work, and also offers help in all practical crafts such as weaving, sewing and writing. Athena will aid you in being able to take on responsibility, to be in a position of power and to use it wisely.

Justice and Wisdom Spell

Aim: To obtain a fair and just outcome in your situation, to gain wisdom as to the best way to resolve an issue.

Tools: Photo or statue of Athena, tea light and holder, frankincense incense, parchment or plain paper, pen.

Create a sacred space as detailed in Chapter One. Light the tealight and place it in front of a photo or statue of Athena.

Light your incense and call upon the Goddess and say:

"Great Goddess Athena, I call to you, Goddess of Justice, Goddess of Wisdom and rational thought. Be present here at this rite and hear my

SUCCESS AND ABUNDANCE

> *Weave* for me a fabric of life
> On your loom of divine power
> Weave into it I ask, your strength as *warrior*,
> Your *wisdom* as counsellor,
> Your *justice* as law giver
> And your skills as craftswoman,
> I ask this blessing of you,
> Great Athena, Goddess divine. *(ii)*

spell. I ask that you imbue my words with your divine power, that I may receive divine justice and the blessings of your wisdom. Great Goddess Athena, I bid you hail and welcome!"

      Close your eyes and visualise the Goddess coming forward and entering into the picture or statue. Open your eyes, and write down on your parchment what it is that you need Athena's help with. Perhaps it is a situation at work; or a situation where you feel you have been treated unfairly and you wish to receive justice; perhaps you need to gain some wisdom and insight into your situation. Read aloud what you have written, and ask Athena to bring about a successful resolution for you. Now close your eyes and meditate on your questions and see what comes to your mind. Perhaps an image, or a solution presents itself. Open your eyes and thank the Goddess for her presence, and bid her: "Hail and farewell!" Take your parchment and roll it up, and place it on an altar in front of Athena for one month. Take note how your situation unfolds during this time. Also, write down any dreams that you have that shed light on your situation, whether during sleep or meditations.

SUCCESS AND ABUNDANCE

Nike

O powerful Nike, thee I invoke, whose might alone can quell
Contending rage and opposing forces fell.
'Tis thine in battle to *confer the crown*,
The *victor's prize*, the mark of sweet renown;
For thou rulest all things, Nike divine!
And *glorious strife*, and joyful shouts are thine.
Come, mighty Goddess, and thy supplicant bless,
With sparkling eyes, *elated with success*;
May deeds illustrious thy protection claim,
And find, led on by thee, immortal fame. *(iii)*

Nike is the Greek Goddess of Success and Victory, who was also known as Victoria in Rome. She is depicted as a strongly built young female, the epitome of physical strength whilst also displaying the gracefulness of a ballerina. Nike is always shown with large wings because she gives people the ability to soar and fly to their heights; to reach for the stars in their aspirations. She is also shown holding a laurel wreath on her arm, the laurel wreath being the accolade, which was bestowed upon the champions of the Olympic Games in ancient Greece, long before the introduction of precious metal medals. Today Nike remains the Goddess of the Olympics, there is an image of her on the back of every medal given out at the Olympic Games. Success in the games encompasses everything that Nike stands for; success and victory against the competition through fair play; being the best you can be and even competing in more than one event. These strong links with physical strength and success in competition led her to be adopted as the name for the leading sports company.

The human experience of victory can manifest in many ways; a general leading an army would feel victorious when he sees his enemy defeated, witnesses the celebrations of his soldiers and when he shares that sense of exhilaration. But victory can also manifest as the aspiration to succeed in one's own endeavours, especially in competitive fields, such as business and sport. It is within Nike's powers to decide the outcome of battles, wars, and all areas of competition, especially sports.

Working with Nike can be very effective when also working with Athena, as one might seek a good strategy when facing a 'battle' or challenging competitive situation. There must always be a winner and a loser in any competition and it is the Goddess Nike who decides who that should be. In mythology Nike flew around battlefields rewarding the victors with glory and fame. Subsequently, the Goddess Athena is often shown holding Nike, 'Success and Victory', in her hand.

All is not lost for those who are defeated, as Nike is the inspiration behind the saying, 'It is not the winning, it is the taking part that counts'. When facing competitive challenges today, it is important to remember that if one had not taken part, then there would have been no chance of winning at all. Defeat may not be pleasant, but it can inspire the loser towards higher aspirations, towards further training and betterment of themselves. Therefore defeat is not an empty experience as it can also lead onto greater victory at a later date.

Working with Nike can help you to achieve your aspirations: whether you need to further improve your skills, to 'go into training', or whether you need to have the confidence to become the best that you can be, the 'best in your field'. Perhaps you need to balance equally your focus between more than one demanding area of your life, 'to compete in more than one event'; perhaps you need to have self-confidence and resolve in the face of opposition, to stand up for yourself and to be heard. Nike is a good Goddess to work with to help you to achieve any of these attributes.

Recipe for Success Spell and Visualisation

Aim: To increase your resolve and confidence; to obtain insight into how to fulfil your potential.
Tools: Statue or photo of Nike, tea light candle and holder, gold, silver and bronze candles (or paint white candles), three candlesticks (a triple candelabra would be ideal), three pieces of paper, pen, frankincense incense, frankincense oil.

SUCCESS AND ABUNDANCE

It is helpful to place the three candlesticks at slightly different heights, with the highest being in the centre, and the other two positioned either side of the it at slightly lower heights. If you cannot obtain a candelabra, then try to position the candles on objects that create differing heights, whilst remembering that safety is of utmost importance and that the candles need to be safe and secure.

Create a sacred space as detailed in Chapter One. Light the tea light and place it in front of the image of the Goddess and call upon her, say:

"Glorious Nike, Queen of Flight. I call upon thee to bless me in my glorious strife, that I may be victorious and renowned for success in my endeavours and wear the victor's crown. Great Goddess Nike, I bid you hail and welcome."

Close your eyes and visualise a golden winged Goddess coming into the room and entering into the image on your altar. When you feel ready, open your eyes and address her. Take the gold candle and tell Nike about the area or situation that you would most love to be successful in. Detail the challenges and why you want to be successful at this. Anoint the candle with frankincense oil and as you light it from the tea light, say: "So mote it be!" Place a piece of blank paper in front of the gold candle.

Repeat the same process with the silver candle as you tell Nike about the second most desired area that you wish to be successful in. Once again, anoint the candle and as you light it say: "So mote it be!" Place it in the second candlestick to one side of the gold, but preferably slightly lower in height. Place a blank piece of paper in front of the silver candle.

Repeat the process a third time with the bronze candle and tell the Goddess about the third most important area that you wish to succeed in, anoint and light the candle and place it in the third candlestick with the words: "So mote it be!" Place the third piece of paper before the bronze candle.

Close your eyes and imagine you are in the amphitheatre of the Ancient Greek Olympic Games. Around you are many athletes all practising for their forthcoming events. Towards you walks a tall, strong woman, dressed in a simple white robe and emanating a golden glow, with beautiful wings. As she approaches you, she smiles and encourages you to walk with her. Together you wander through the amphitheatre, observing the athletes, focussed and intent upon their training, practising and preparing for the forthcoming games. Walk with her awhile, tell her about your three goals and listen to the advice that she gives you: perhaps she gives you

SUCCESS AND ABUNDANCE

tips on how to improve your performance in your chosen fields; perhaps it is to give up certain habits or activities which are holding you back; or to approach your aspirations by an altogether different route. Take note of what she tells you. Nike leads you to the beginning of a race, where the athletes are lined up ready to start and invites you to take your place in the line up. As the signal is given, you find yourself racing forwards, your heart pounding with exhilaration as you fly forwards towards your goal. The finish line is in sight and your feel yourself flying with the speed of the Goddess, as if you too had wings, your feet hardly touching the ground. With a great sense of joy, you cross the finish line in first place, the victorious winner. How do you feel? Perhaps you are surprised at yourself, at your ability to achieve. The crowds cheer and you are guided to the podium, where Nike awaits. She invites you to take your place and places a laurel wreath upon your head and a gold medal around your neck. Close your eyes as you listen to your heart and feel the true sense of victory, of achievement, in the knowledge that you have achieved your best because you deserved it, because you are the best in your field.

    Slowly bring your awareness back into your body and wiggle your toes. In your own time open your eyes. Take the pieces of paper in front of each candle and write down the advice that Nike gave you to help you to achieve each goal. Also write down any other impressions that come to you in relation to each wish. Let your candles burn all the way down and keep the pieces of paper safely until you have achieved your three goals, re-reading them each time you wish to reaffirm your intentions.

SUCCESS AND ABUNDANCE

The Goddess of Good Fortune
Fortuna
By Markus Wolfson

Great Goddess Fortuna, thee we invoke,

that you may bestow upon us the *luck and joy* that we seek.

Spin your *Wheel of Fortune* for us this night

and may your blessings be ever bright.

Your Horn of Plenty doth overflow and *nourish us* that we may grow.

Guide us to greet the golden dawn of opportunity by your grace foretold.

Fortuna is the Roman Goddess of Abundance and Good Fortune, often referred to as Our Lady Good Fortune. Her main cult was around Praeneste (modern Palestrina) about 20 miles east of Rome, and at Antium (modern Anzio) on the coast about 20 miles to the south. The temple known to have existed at Antium has never been discovered, but the remains of a magnificent temple are to be found at Praeneste, where her oracle told the fortunes of supplicants which were inscribed on tablets known as the Praenestine lots. Contemporary with the remains of the earliest worship of Fortuna, archaeologists have discovered ancient bronze and ivory caskets with words written on them in Etruscan and an archaic form of Latin. Her worship goes back to the time when the Latin people were ruled by the Etruscans, about the seventh century B.C. Her Etruscan name was Nortia.

"Primigenia" – "First Bearer"– was the cult name of Fortuna at Praeneste. She was called this because she was the mother of other Gods, including Jupiter and Juno. In the temple there was a statue of her holding the twin infants Jupiter and Juno in her arms. She was also a protector of women in childbirth.

There is a connection between Fortuna and Neptunus (Neptune), the God of the Sea and of the Unconscious, and the dreaming mind. Fortuna carries a steering oar, the ancient equivalent of a rudder, symbolic of her power to guide mortals through life, and obviously connected to the sea and ships. The horn of plenty, which she also carries, is a large sea-shell.

The fishermen and sailors of ancient Antium back in the Etruscan period worshipped her as a patron Goddess and protectress. Around five hundred years afterwards, in the second century B.C., a mosaic pavement was laid in the temple of Fortuna Primigenia at Praeneste, illustrating a temple of Neptunus by the sea, in which swim an abundance of fish.

These two important functions, protectress of seamen and of women giving birth, that Fortuna had in early times, were perhaps partly the reason why at a later period she was sometimes identified with Diana Lucina, also a Goddess of Childbirth. She was also associated with the moon, Lady Luna, who clearly had domain over the tides; and Isis, the Egyptian mother Goddess, in the Roman period a protectress of pregnant women and sailors.

In modern times, Neptune also presides over the deep mysterious ocean of the unconscious. The personal ego can drown in it, but it is also the source of inspiration and wisdom: 'the pearl of great price'. Fortuna can guide the aspirant, so that he or she can attain the wisdom, and avoid the dangers lurking in the murky depths. With Fortuna's help it is possible to develop lucid dreaming and astral travel, clairvoyance and mediumistic powers.

The appearance of a deity was widely understood to be symbolic of her nature. The three attributes of Fortuna are: the steering-oar, the ancient equivalent of the rudder; the cornucopia, a Latin word meaning horn of plenty, a large sea-shell filled with fruit; and the Wheel of Fortune, an eight-spoked wheel.

The steering oar is symbolic of the power Fortuna has to steer her votary through life, ensuring that he or she reaches safe havens and avoids the rocks. The cornucopia reminds the supplicant that Fortuna has the power to grant abundance of all good things to those who please her. The wheel of fortune represents the change of the seasons, the life-cycle, the cycle of the births and deaths of the reincarnating soul, and, more mundanely, the ups and downs of life.

Fortuna is a wonderful, generous deity, and rewards everyone who worships her. When Fortuna loves you she will change your destiny and bring you great good fortune. If you're in need of good luck, or doors opening on new opportunities for fulfilment; if you're not sure what to do, and feel in need of divine guidance; if your life is characterised by want and lack rather than the wonderful abundance that you have a right to – then Fortuna is the Goddess for you. Fortuna will also bless you if you're bringing a new child into the world, or launching a new project. And she will protect you on long journeys – and give you the powers of astral travel, clairvoyance and mediumship.

One way to gain the blessings of the Goddess is to contact her in your imagination by visualising her. This exercise enables you to access Fortuna energy, and just by practising it, even if you make no special request, it will change your luck for the better. Repeat it every day for as

long as you feel you want to. As well as good fortune in the form of external events, because of her power to guide, Fortuna will give you hunches, intuitions, good ideas that seem to come from nowhere. Be prepared to recognise these and act on them.

Visualisation

Create a sacred space as detailed in Chapter One. Close your eyes.

You are the captain of an Ancient Roman ship, with five banks of oars on either side, sailing on the calm and beautiful blue Mediterranean. A cool breeze fills the sails. You hear the sea birds cry, and smell the salt spray. A hot sun beats down on the decks. You are not far from land – to the starboard you can see white foam breaking on white sand, which rises to the grey-green wooded hills of Italy.

The weather changes. The sky grows overcast and black; the wind gets up; the waves mount up and lash against the sides of the ship; soon the sails are rags torn by the wind, and the ship is tossed about like flotsam. In the gloom it is impossible to see where a safe haven lies – from horizon to horizon all you can see are the foam-flecked tops of furious dark waves. You feel greatly afraid.

You pray to Neptune, God of the Sea, and to Fortuna, she who guides the steering oar. Lady Fortuna appears at the stern of the ship, holding the steering oar; she smiles at you, and all at once your fear dissolves; you know, with absolute certainty, that now she is present nothing can harm you, or your crew.

She guides you, in spite of the tempest, to an off-shore island. There is a cove sheltered from the winds, and you are able to heave to, and lay anchor there. Now she walks towards you, and, as she does so, you realise how tall she is: as tall as the tallest mast on the ship. She looks down at you, and it seems that light and fire flash from her eyes, and, at that moment, any wish that you have will be granted.

You make your wish; and at that moment the weather abates; mysteriously, the grey skies disappear, the sea returns to a brilliant blue, the hot Mediterranean sun beats on the decks once more. You order new sails to be run up; you weigh anchor and set sail; you sail over calm seas, and soon find yourself in harbour at Antium, your port of destination. When you are ready, bring your awareness back into your body and open your eyes.

A Spell to Make and Manifest the Right Choice

This spell will help you decide which choice to make, and, at the same time, it will help to bring the best possible outcome into manifestation. For example, suppose you want to train for a new job, but you can't decide which course of study to take – whether it should be, let's suppose, Office Management, Interior Design, or the Beauty Industry. The spell will help you decide, and also ensure that you get a good exam result at the end of your course!

Draw a large circle on an A4 (8.5"x11") piece of paper and divide it into as many equal parts as you have choices before you. In the example above, that would be three. Then draw symbols of success for the possible outcomes, or if appropriate, you might cut pictures out of magazines and stick them in the space in the circle designated for that particular choice. As well as, or instead of that, you could write the desired outcome in a short phrase or sentence in your best handwriting, again in the appropriate section of the circle. Using the example above, for instance, you might write "Top marks in my Office Management exam" "Top marks in my Interior Design exam", "Top marks in my Beauty Industry exam".

To make a choice you need a pendulum. You can buy one from a shop specialising in New Age and Pagan books and equipment, or make one yourself by tying a small weight to a length of string, or use a necklace with a crystal drop pendant. Hold the pendulum in your left hand and say: "Give me a 'Yes'." The pendulum will eventually begin to move, either back and forth, from side to side, or round in a clockwise or anti-clockwise circle. However it moves, that means "Yes". Then still the pendulum and say: "Give me a 'No'." In the same way, find out what movement of the pendulum means "No".

You also need some flowers, preferably: irises, pansies, gladioli, or sunflowers; four purple or blue candles; a picture or statue of Fortuna; some of your favourite biscuits on a plate; some wine and a wine glass; and some incense.

Now you've gathered together all the equipment you need for the spell, you're ready to begin. Arrange to have some time out, free of the demands of family, friends and work. Create a sacred space as described in Chapter One. Then approach the altar and raising your hands, recite the hymn quoted below, or, if you prefer, words of your own making:

"Lady Fortuna, Oracle of Praeneste, hear me!"
"Lady Fortuna, Mother of the Gods, hear me!"
"Lady Fortuna, who bears the steering oar, guide me!"
"Lady Fortuna, who bears the cornucopia, grant me prosperity!"
"Lady Fortuna, who guards the Wheel of Fortune, grant me happiness!"
"Lady Fortuna, be with me now!"

Then say: "Gracious Lady, you who hold the steering oar and the cornucopia, guardian of the wheel of fortune, deign to instruct through the pendulum which of the possible choices will make me the happiest."

You might want to put the sentiment in your own words, of course, but avoid using such words as "should" and "ought to", because they don't mean anything here. The important thing is what makes you happy, not what some other person might believe you should do.

Then hold the pendulum over each of the partitions you have drawn, and ask the question, "Is this the best choice for me?" Over one, the pendulum will say "Yes".

If it so happens that the pendulum says "Yes" to more than one, that probably means that you would be equally happy with either or all of those choices. In that case, hold the pendulum over each of the choices in turn that, according to the pendulum, would make you happy, and say: "Gracious Lady Fortuna, of those choices that make me happy, do you prefer me to do this one?"

Almost certainly you will get a single "Yes" after doing this. If you still get an ambiguous result, there may be something wrong with your choices, so there would be a need to reassess them. Very likely, there's another option that you've forgotten about, which is preferable to any of those you have considered. The same is true if the pendulum says "No" to all your choices.

When Fortuna has shown you the best choice, pour out some wine into the glass, and raising it up, say: "Bless this offering to you, Fortuna, and endow it with your power."
Drink some of the wine, then say: "Fortuna manifests my will. The right choice will come into my life."

Place the wine glass, and the rest of the wine, on the altar, saying: "Lady Fortuna, accept this offering."

Do the same with the biscuits, eating one, and offering the rest to Fortuna.

Then say, if the pendulum has indicated a definite outcome: "Thank you, Lady Fortuna, for manifesting my will." If the pendulum has not given you a definite outcome, say: "Thank you, Lady Fortuna, for giving me the guidance which will allow my future choice to come into manifestation."

You have now done all you need to do. The ceremony is finished. You can eat and drink the rest of the wine and biscuits after the ceremony if you like.

Fortuna was an Ancient Roman Goddess, but as with many Roman Goddesses, she had an equivalent in Ancient Greece. The Greek equivalent was Tyche, which means 'Lady Luck'. As she is also the Goddess of Divination, she is often depicted holding a scrying bowl, the ancient equivalent of a crystal ball. Tyche was not reckoned as one of the twelve Olympians, so to make up for that, the Greeks identified her with Artemis, as well as Hecate and the Moon (Selene).

SUCCESS AND ABUNDANCE

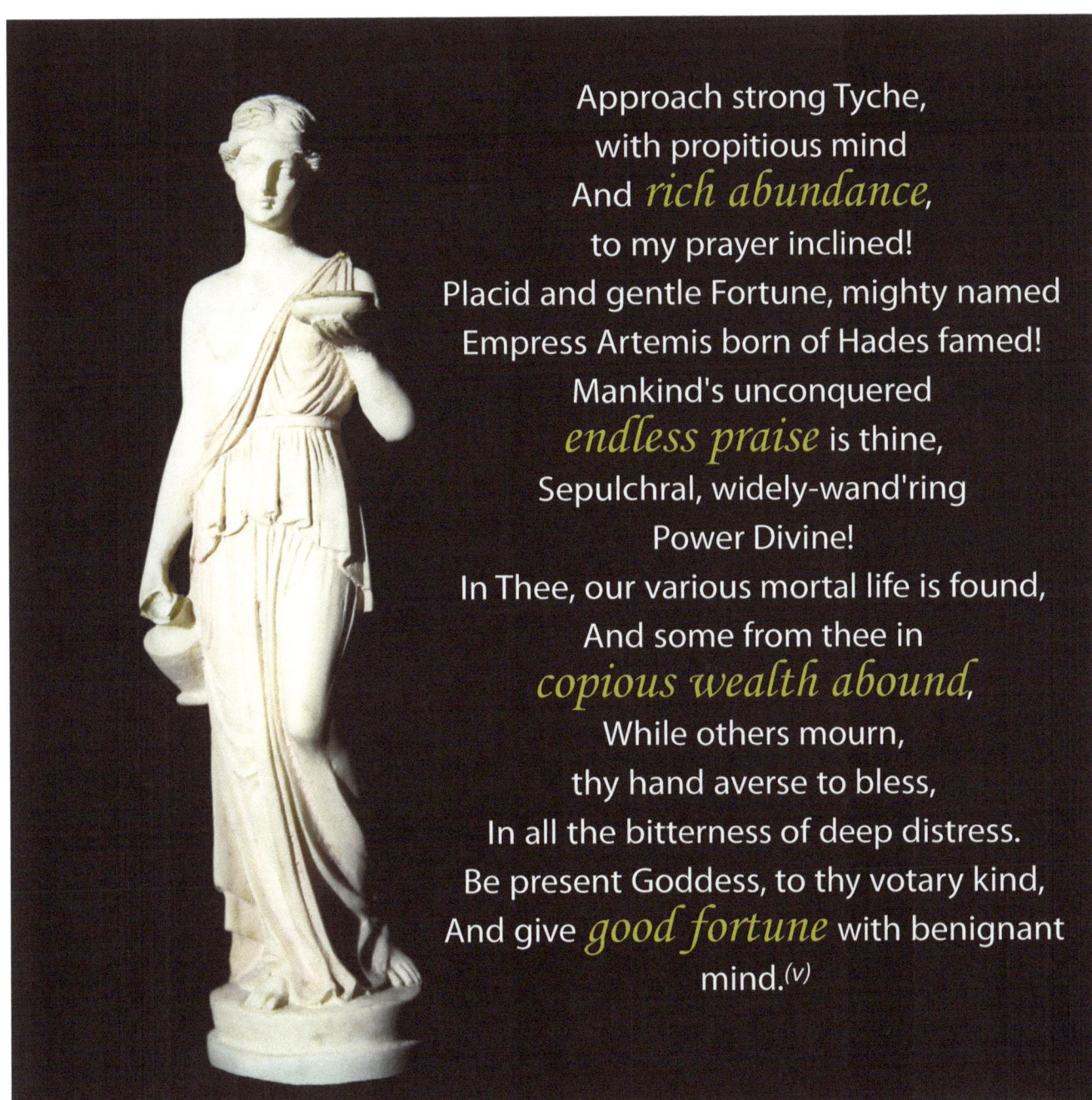

Approach strong Tyche,
with propitious mind
And *rich abundance*,
to my prayer inclined!
Placid and gentle Fortune, mighty named
Empress Artemis born of Hades famed!
Mankind's unconquered
endless praise is thine,
Sepulchral, widely-wand'ring
Power Divine!
In Thee, our various mortal life is found,
And some from thee in
copious wealth abound,
While others mourn,
thy hand averse to bless,
In all the bitterness of deep distress.
Be present Goddess, to thy votary kind,
And give *good fortune* with benignant
mind.(v)

Working with Athena, Nike, and Fortuna Together

Athena, Nike and Fortuna are three Goddesses who harmonise very well and working with them together can result in some very powerful magic.

If it is success in work that you want, then you first ask Athena for skilled judgement and wisdom. This helps to you to fine tune your intentions, to think through a plan or ambition, so that you do not embark upon a course of action recklessly. Athena provides you with the wisdom and strategy to calculate a way to proceed with successful results. After all, what use are good intentions if they are not followed though with decisive and effective action?

When Nike is added into the equation, she is a Goddess who will guide us towards success and victory in our endeavours; to help us to excel, to be the best that we can be and to win against the competition or any opposition that we may encounter. If our aspirations require us to improve our skills, to learn new things or to improve in any way, then Nike can help us to 'go into training', to become the best that we can be and even identify our strengths and specialisms. Nike can also help us to multi-task as she can help us to do well in more than one area.

Add Fortuna to the mix and your spell is complete. It is good for us to focus our Will, to be clear in our intentions, but sometimes this can lead to our being too single minded. It is good to maintain an attitude where one is open to opportunity, whilst at the same time being focussed upon one's intentions. This is not always easy, as it may seem that one is required to do two contradictory things at the same time. This is where Fortuna comes in, as the Goddess of Good Luck and Fortune, she helps maintain an element of spontaneity in the situation, and helps us to remain open to the possibility of our intentions manifesting in a way that we might not have envisaged. If we are too single minded, we might miss out on golden opportunities. Fortuna keeps this door open and helps us to be in the right place at the right time. This element of chance is often necessary for our dreams to manifest.

Visualisation / Ritual

Aim: To bring about success, justice and good fortune in business and career issues.
Tools: Statues / photos of Athena, Nike and Fortuna, three tea lights and holders, one for each Goddess, small glass for each Goddess. Green, gold, and purple candles, candlesticks.
Incense: Frankincense.
Oils: Bergamot, Frankincense, Sandalwood.
Offerings: Wine, flowers.

Prepare a sacred space as detailed in Chapter One. Light your incense, and place the tea lights in their holders, one in front of each Goddess. Call upon the Goddesses: light the tea light in front of Athena and say:

"I call to you Athena, great Goddess of Wisdom, Goddess of War and Justice. You, who lead the armies like a general, who are successful in battle due to your good strategy and planning. Great Athena, you carry a sword and shield to fight your enemies, but you do not need to raise them as you hold the Goddess Nike in your hand, Goddess of Success and Victory. Grant us your wisdom and strategy in our battles, our challenges. Goddess of Working Women, of the Arts and Writing, help us in our chosen professions, that we maybe inspired and find joy within our work. Great Goddess Athena, we bid you hail and welcome!"

Light the tea light in front of Nike and say:

"Great Goddess Nike, we call to you who are the Goddess of Success and Victory, of the Olympic Games. Grant us success in our endeavours, enable us to be the best in our field, and if we should find ourselves needing to develop our skills further, then we ask that you grant us the ability to train and excel in our chosen areas. As the Olympic athletes train to compete by the code of fair play and good sportsmanship, we ask that we achieve success and victory in our careers though fair play and gain reward through our excellence. If there are areas that we need to improve, let us be aware of them and better ourselves as needed. Great Goddess Nike, we bid you, hail and welcome!"

Light the tea light in front of Fortuna and say:

"Great Goddess Fortuna, Goddess of Fortune and Opportunity, help us to be open to opportunities, to think on our feet and respond to unexpected developments. Grant us the good fortune to be in the right place at the right time, meet the right people and follow the right leads to further our careers, so that we may enjoy the abundance of your cornucopia as it overflows with prosperity. Great Goddess Fortuna, we bid you hail and welcome!"

Close your eyes and see yourself at the foot of a hill, in an arid landscape, with groves of olive trees on the hillside around you. As you look towards the top of the hill you see the Acropolis, with its white marble pillars gleaming in the warm sun. Start to walk up the hill towards the temple, and as you arrive you step out of the heat into the cool shade. You can see a water fountain, and an owl perched nearby, hooting gently. You walk across the courtyard towards a figure seated on a marble bench, reading a book. A sword and shield rest alongside her. This is Athena, Goddess of Wisdom and Justice. Sit with her awhile and seek her advice. Tell her what it is you would wish for.

The owl takes flight and you look up, the sound of wings beating in the breeze. It is not the owl that you hear, you look up to see a great winged Goddess approach you from the side of the temple, with her huge white wings held aloft. Behold Nike, the Goddess of Success and Victory wearing a laurel wreath upon her arm. She smiles at you, and you see her physical prowess, her strength of body and will. You approach her, and ask her if there is anything that you can do to help yourself become better in your chosen field, to become a better competitor, to become a winner. Stay with her awhile.

You hear a movement behind you, a sound of something spinning, whirring, and you turn to see another Goddess in the courtyard, a beautiful Goddess in a purple robe, with a wheel spinning beside her, the Wheel of Fortune. In her left arm she cradles the overflowing abundant cornucopia, and in her right hand she holds the oar by which she will steer your fate. Behold Fortuna, Goddess of Fortune and Opportunity. Speak with her awhile, and ask her for good luck and opportunities; to be in the right place at the right time; to call the right people at the right moment; and to accept opportunity when it comes to you, even if it is unexpected. As the three Goddesses gather round you, they each give you a gift and final words of guidance. You thank the Goddesses and take your leave of them, safe in the knowledge that you may return to see them at any time. You walk back across the courtyard, and step once again back out into the heat of the sun and begin your descent of the hill, walking through the olive groves, until you find yourself walking into a bright light. As you walk through the light, you find yourself back in the room and see yourself sat in front of your altar with the Goddesses and candles in front of them. Bring your awareness back into your body and wiggle your toes, and in your own time open your eyes.

Focus once again upon your altar and the statues or photos of the three Goddesses and address them, offer them a glass of wine and a flower, and as you do so you ask them once again for what you would like them to help you with. Then take your gold candle and anoint it with bergamot oil, focus upon the candle and ask for the ability to shine, to be the best that you can be, to excel in your chosen field. Light the candle from the flame in front of Nike and say: "So mote it be!" Place the candle in the candlestick. Take your green candle and anoint it with frankincense oil, focus on it and ask that you may have work that inspires you and that you can excel in. Ask that your working life be abundant, that you may earn more than enough money than you need, and that it comes to you effortlessly, by doing work that you thoroughly enjoy. Light the candle from the flame in front of Athena and say: "So mote it be!" Place the candle in the candlestick. Now take your purple candle and anoint it with sandalwood oil. Focus on your candle, and ask for opportunities and good fortune, to be in the right place at the right time. Ask to be open to your desires manifesting in an unexpected way, and for the ability to be able to recognise good opportunities when they present themselves. If you are applying for a job, ask for good luck when being interviewed, if you are self-employed, ask for more business to come your way. Ask for these opportunities to lead to greater abundance. Light the candle from the flame in front of Fortuna and say: "So mote it be!" Place the candle in the candlestick. Sit a while in front of your altar and see if any more thoughts or inspirations come to you. Thank the Goddesses for their help and bid them: "Hail and farewell!"

Let your candles burn all the way down.

Abundance Altar

SUCCESS AND ABUNDANCE

Abundance Altar

GODDESSES OF TRANSFORMATION
Hecate

I invoke you, beloved Hecate of the Crossroads and the Three Ways,
Goddess of the heavens and the *Underworld,*
Tomb-frequenter, who dwells in mysterious realms with the souls of the dead,
Nightgoing One, greet us at the Threshold,
Unconquerable Queen of compelling countenance,
Keyholding mistress of the whole world.
You are ruler, Nymph, Mountain wandering *nurturer of youth.*
Maiden, I beg you to be present at these sacred rites. (i)

Hecate is the Goddess of the Crossroads, depicted as three Goddesses joined together at the back, a triple aspect Goddess. She was worshipped at the crossroads, which in ancient times was the meeting of three ways not four. People were very superstitious about the crossroads as they believed that here lay the gateway between this world and the Underworld, and that crossroads were haunted by ghosts. Although Hecate is mainly associated with the Graeco-Roman pantheon, her origins date back to Chaldean times. She is so ancient, that historians find it hard to identify exactly when she began to be worshipped and by whom, as she has been adopted by many cultures over the centuries. Hecate is sometimes represented as an Earth Goddess and also as a Moon Goddess.

Hecate was known as a Goddess who would grant wishes, so people would make offerings to her at the crossroads. They would leave a cake surrounded by lit torches at the centre of the crossroads as they made their wish and then they would walk away, without looking back. The cake would then be eaten by wolves, or according to some versions of the

 myth, they would be eaten by the poor. These offerings were known as 'Hecate's Suppers'. [ii] This tradition of serving a cake surrounded by lit torches, known as an amphiphon, has survived today and forms the origins of our tradition of the birthday cake with candles on top. Ancient cakes would be made from pearl barley and honey, with spices such as cinnamon. Historians disagree as to the time of the month when Hecate's suppers were offered to her. Many cite that it was on the day before the new moon, the dark moon, as this was the day that Hecate emerged from Hades. Other accounts detail that she was honoured on the thirtieth day of every month, but as the Greek calendar was lunar, it is likely that the thirtieth of each month was the dark moon. However, there are also many accounts that also tell of her being honoured on the thirteenth of every month, on the full moon. It is quite possible that the tradition of worshipping her on the full moon was adopted from rites to Artemis, and became associated with Hecate at a later date. So we find her associated with both of these moon phases and we can work with her at either time.

Hecate's annual festival in Greece was on August the 13th and at this time worshippers asked Hecate for her help and protection for their crops from the fierce storms that would often occur at this time and were believed to be caused by the Moon.

Hecate's three main aspects are Goddess of Sorcery and Magic; Goddess of Intuition and Madness; and Goddess of the Dead and Transformation, and it is this aspect that shall be dealt with in this volume. For other aspects of Hecate, please refer to *Volume One: Goddesses of the Seasons*.

GODDESSES OF TRANSFORMATION

Hecate's primary totem animal is the wolf or wild dog and her presence was signified by the barking of dogs. Some accounts describe Hecate as being accompanied by ghostly dogs and others tell of her hounds emerging from the Underworld.

Hecate's other totem animal is the snake and she is often depicted with serpents at her feet. They represent transformation and rebirth as they shed their skins. When working with Hecate, you can ask for transformation on a personal level, by 'shedding your skin', your old persona, your old habits, attitudes and so on, and thereby changing yourself. You can also ask for transformation in your external life, as you stand at the crossroads, by asking Hecate to guide you as to which path to take. This can help you to change direction in your life and bring about your desires. Be aware that as you cross the crossroads, you really can alter the course of your life, so as the wise old saying goes: 'Be careful what you wish for'.

Be aware also, that as the Goddess of Sorcery and Magic, and known as the granter of wishes, Hecate's magic is strong and powerful, so do not approach her if you intend to change your mind the following day. She is not a Goddess for the flippant.

Another aspect of Hecate is the Goddess of the Dead. She dwells in the Underworld, illuminating the way through the darkness for those who have died, guiding their way through the Underworld and on to the Afterlife. She does this with the aid of two flaming torches, which she holds aloft, casting light in the darkness. So, in everyday life we find that Hecate is the Goddess we can turn to when someone dies or when

GODDESSES OF TRANSFORMATION

GODDESSES OF TRANSFORMATION

we wish to ask for a blessing for the deceased. We can also find solace for the bereaved, for those who find themselves in a place of darkness brought about by their grief. Hecate's torches can be used to shed light and illuminate a path ahead for those that do not know which way to turn, for those facing a metaphoric 'death' in the form of dramatic change in their lives as they illuminate the Unconscious and reveal hidden knowledge. Hecate is depicted holding several symbols in her hands: a key, representing the key to the Underworld, as well as opening the doors of new opportunities; a rope, representing the Mortal Coil; and a dagger with which to cut the Mortal Coil.

Visualisation / Ritual on the Dark or Full Moon

Aim: To ask for a wish to be granted, to bring about change in your life and yourself.
Tools: Statue or picture of Hecate, tea light candle and holder to illuminate the statue. A cake (preferably dark chocolate), birthday candles, frankincense incense, silver and orange candles, candlesticks.

Prepare a sacred space as detailed in Chapter One. Light your candle in front of the Goddess and your incense. Call upon the Goddess Hecate and say:
"Great Goddess Hecate I call upon you, Goddess of the Crossroads, of the Three Ways, you who stand at the threshold between this world and the next, Triple Goddess, Goddess of Sorcery, I ask that you be here and bless my spell with your magic, Goddess of Intuition, and also Madness and Delusion, I ask that my intentions be inspired and protected, that I may retain clarity of mind.

Goddess of Transformation and Death, I ask to shed my old skin, that which I no longer desire, and embrace the new paths that you offer to me. Goddess of the Crossroads, hear my spell and grant my wish. Hail Hecate! Hail Hecate! Hail Hecate!"

Then take the silver candle, and as you hold it, address the Goddess and ask her what you want. Light the candle from the tea light in front of the statue and say: "So mote it be!" Place the candle securely in a candlestick and take the orange candle. As you hold it, address the Goddess and ask for the confidence, courage and energy to take the action required to achieve your desires and to allow change to come into your life. Light the candle and place in a candlestick. Place one candle on each side of your statue, to represent her two flaming torches.

Now sit or lie in front of the altar and close your eyes. Be aware of the light upon your altar from the light before the statue and the two candles, one on each side of her. In your mind's eye, you see yourself approaching a crossroads, and as you do you see her, standing where the path meets two others, a meeting of three ways. A triple Goddess, appearing as three women who are joined together at the back, stands before you next to a tree, barren of leaves, whose roots are entwined around the headstones of timeless graves. Serpents slither at her feet, and in her hands she holds two flaming torches, a rope, a key, and two daggers. Fearsome, compelling and yet beautiful, you approach her by the light of the full moon. Hecate invites you to come forward and ask for what you desire. Voice your fears if you have any, tell her of your concerns. Then listen to the advice she gives you, and take note of which path she indicates for you to follow. You thank her and walk across the crossroads and along your path. You walk down the path and find yourself re-entering the room and see where you are sat or lying before your altar. Bring your awareness back into your body by wiggling your toes and open your eyes.

Now arrange the birthday candles upon the cake in the pattern of a three way crossroads, light the candles and offer the cake to Hecate. Place it before the statue and say:
"Great Goddess Hecate, I offer you this cake, lit by candles representing the crossroads whereupon you stand. Please accept this offering from me and grant me my desires." Blow the candles out before they set fire to the cake, unless you like your chocolate singed! And serve yourself some cake in her honour. Let your silver and orange candles burn all the way down.

GODDESSES OF TRANSFORMATION

GODDESSES OF TRANSFORMATION

Arianrhod

Arianrhod of the *Silver Wheel*,
by all the names men give thee, we, thy hidden children,
humbly ask thy truth to hear,
thy countenance to see.
Here in the circle cast upon the Earth,
yet open to the *stars*, unseen, we call to you.
Within our hearts give understanding birth,
our wounds of loss and loneliness do heal.
Goddess of the *Dawn* and Stars
may our dreams and hopes *soar unto the heights*.
With you, *Moon Mother*,
the Wheel doth turn,
to you Great Mother do we all return. *(iii)*

Arianrhod is a Celtic Goddess of Transformation, associated with the ancient Welsh people and she is depicted as holding a silver wheel, that turns as your life changes. She is the Goddess of the Moon, the Stars and the Dawn as well as the Corona Borealis. The silver wheel that she holds represents the turning wheel of all transformation and change, including reincarnation. Her sacred animal is the owl.

Among the Ancient Welsh people, there was a curious custom for the King to sit with his feet in the lap of a virgin. According to myth, Math the Lord of Gwynedd was told by his foot-holder, Goewin, that she had been raped by his nephews, Gwydyon and Gilvaethwy, and so could no longer perform this function for him. He was advised to select, as a replacement,

GODDESSES OF TRANSFORMATION

Arianrhod, daughter of Don, of whom it was written: "The glory of Arianrhod's looks exceeds summer dawn", so he sent for her. Asked if she were a virgin, she replied: "I know not, Lord, other than that I am." As a test he held out his magic wand and told her to step over it. She did so, and promptly two children dropped from her. One, with yellow hair, was baptised Dylan, meaning 'sea', but the other boy, whom Gwydyon (who was apparently his father) had nursed by a nursemaid, was initially nameless. Arianrhod was very angry that her secret had been revealed and that everyone now knew that she wasn't a virgin. She vowed that the boy would have no name unless she gave him one.

Gwydyon raised the boy and then later posed as a shoemaker with his son as his apprentice. They sailed to Arianrhod's castle, Caer Arianrhod, which was located on an island, off the coast of Caernarfon. Arianrhod didn't recognise them as they talked to her about making her some shoes. The boy aimed an arrow at a wren that alighted on their ship, and hit it in the leg. Arianrhod said: "The light-haired one hit it with a skilful hand." She had unwittingly given him a name, and he became known as Llew Llaw Gyffes, 'Bright one of the Skilful Hand'. Realising that she had been deceived, Arianrhod swore that the boy would have no weapons until she armed him herself.

After that Llew was trained in horsemanship and Gwydyon took him again to Caer Arianrhod. This time they posed as bards. The next day Gywdyon used his magic to create the illusion of a fleet of ships surrounding the castle. Arianrhod handed out weapons to everyone present, but once she had armed Llew, Gwydyon made the ships disappear again. Arianrhod had been tricked once more.

Though the spot in the sea where Caer Arianrhod was supposed to have been located is marked on Ordnance Survey maps, this was on the material plane only. Her true home was in the constellation of Corona Borealis, also known as the 'Crown of the North Wind'. In some interpretations, we find that the name Arianrhod means 'silver crown'. In ancient times, this star group was believed to be the place where the souls of the dead went whilst awaiting reincarnation.

Arianrhod is the Goddess to work with when you are seeking to change the events of your life, when you need the 'wheel to turn' for you. Ask for the intuitive insight that she can give you as a Goddess of the Moon, also for the hope and optimism she can give you as a Goddess of the Stars and the ability to make a fresh start as the Goddess of the Dawn. As the Goddess of Reincarnation, she can help you to reinvent yourself, to pick yourself up and start all over again.

Arianrhod Spell
By Seldiy Bate

Aim: Arianrhod is the Lady of Reincarnation. She does not let go of the past, so for us, when we can't let go of the past, perhaps we need to find out more about what it is that is holding us back and what we can bring forward from it, in order to learn and develop. And this may go into a past life. So use this ritual to connect yourself with a past life and find out why it is important now.

Tools: Photo or statue of Arianrhod, three silver candles, candlesticks, black altar cloth, thirteen silver coloured coins, notebook and pen.

Incense: Perfumes that are connected with the lunar energy are almond, jasmine or ambergris.

Timing: This spell should be conducted on the night of the full moon. You may perform it more than once, but only when the Moon is full. If you wish to work with Arianrhod over the course of the year, to develop your own personal "story", make sure you keep notes.

Create a sacred space as detailed in Chapter One. Set out an altar, spread with a black cloth and light the incense. Place the three silver-coloured candles, in suitable holders and arrange them in a slight arc, so that the middle one is slightly further back than the ones on each side. Take the thirteen silver-coloured coins, these can be mixed values, but should be legal tender, and place them in a pile in the middle of your altar. Have a notebook and pen within reach, as you may find you have something to write down. If you don't get anything there and then, write up your experience later anyway. What you did, what happened or what didn't happen, how you felt, what thoughts occurred to you, etc. Even things that don't immediately seem relevant will make more sense over time, as you go over your notes throughout your progress. Have some low lighting, just enough light to see by. The darker it is, the more you will connect with your hidden side. When you are ready, get plenty of incense going, and light your three candles in a row, left to right. Say:

"Arianrhod, Lady of the Silver Wheel, let me take from the past what I need for the present. To show me who I am and how I may grow In your silver light, Lady of the Turning Wheel!"

Put your hands in the pile of coins, half closing your eyes and keep mixing them until you feel compelled to pull out one, without looking. Feel it first, in your hand. What is your first impression?

Now look at it, spend some time looking at the side that is uppermost. Something will come to you. The picture on the coin is relevant and, if a value is shown, that number will have some meaning.

GODDESSES OF TRANSFORMATION

Don't try too hard, just let it flow. You may hear words, a name, sounds, music, or see an image. Now write any notes before you forget and thank the Goddess in your own way. Extinguish the candles in the same order as you lit them. Keep the special coin and take the rest. Spend them randomly, giving some away.

Visualisation / Ritual

Aim: to bring about change in your life, to fulfil your wishes, to increase your courage and cunning, to turn the wheel to your advantage and to cast your spells with wondrous effect.
Tools: A photo or statue of Arianrhod, green and white candles, bergamot oil for mental alertness and frankincense oil to make a connection with the Goddess, candlesticks, benzoin incense. Citrine for confidence and mental alertness.

Prepare your sacred space as detailed in Chapter One. Light the incense and call upon the Goddess, say: "I call to thee, great Goddess Arianrhod, Goddess of the Moon and Stars, of the Dawn and beauteous wonder of the Corona Borealis. Come forth, O Goddess, with your silver wheel, that I may embrace change in my life with courage in my heart and a cunning mind. Weave your magic for me, great Goddess, that I may come to you as a small child and find comfort in your warm embrace. Great Goddess Arianrhod, I bid you, hail and welcome!"

Anoint your white candle with bergamot oil and light it, place it securely in a candlestick and place your citrine next to it. Anoint your green candle with frankincense and light it, place it securley in a candlestick, and place it next to the white candle. Sit or lie down comfortably and close your eyes. In your mind's eye be aware of the flickering light of the white candle flame, and feel yourself drawn into its light, enveloped in its soft light, its golden glow, embraced by its warmth. See yourself surrounded by light and walking forward through the light, until you find yourself in a silvery blue moonlit landscape. The colour of the sky astounds you with its tones ranging from pink to blue to purple and green. Stars sparkle in the sky as the large full moon sits low in the night sky and shines down upon you. You walk towards the crest of a hill where you see the Goddess sat before you, with a large silver wheel in her arms, spinning gently, first one way and then the other. As you approach her she looks up at you and smiles, welcoming you with her warmth and beauty, the mother, nurturing and all knowing. There is something about her eyes that captivates you, that holds your gaze with a depth and intensity which reminds you of something or someone, you know not what, for it is hard to say where you have seen those eyes before. A fluttering above you causes you to look up into the silvery radiance of the large

full moon. There they are again, those eyes. You remember them now as you meet the piercing gaze of an owl, swooping gracefully towards you, a symbol of power and wisdom. You look once more towards the goddess who is smiling at you, laughing with joy. Here, in her domain, you stand alone with the Goddess and see the wondrous Borealis light up the sky, so vibrant, so alive. She takes your hand and you feel yourself rise up and float amongst the glowing lights and the stars, flying gently through the hazy sea of colours until you find a star gleaming right in front of you, so close, so near to touch. You reach out and touch the star and as you do, say aloud your wish, that which you desire. Hold that star in your hand and feel its exhilarating energy running up your arm and filling you with a magical light. After a while you feel yourself drift gently down once again until your feet land upon the ground, your star safely in your hand. Arianrhod extends her silver wheel towards you. You place your star at the centre of the wheel and it starts to turn. Around and around it spins, creating a vortex of power, until it spins so fast that your star flies up and off into the sky, hurtling into the universe and beyond. As you follow it with your gaze you realise that the sky has changed and that now a beautiful dawn is breaking, the beautiful shades of pink, purple and blue light up the sky as the sun starts to climb up over the horizon. You turn to Arianrhod and thank her for her help, for spinning her wheel and granting your wish and you take your leave, secure in the knowledge that you may return to see her at any time. You walk towards the light of the sun, rising now above the horizon and as you draw closer, its light envelops you, and you find yourself surrounded in a warm, golden glow. As you walk through the light, you find yourself once again back in your room in front of your altar, with your white candle burning brightly. See yourself step back into your body and bring your awareness back gradually. Wiggle your toes and become aware of your breathing, and in your own time open your eyes and say:

"I give thanks to you, Arianrhod, for your guidance and blessings and I ask that you may continue to guide me in my waking life, as I make manifest on the material plane that which has been conceived in the realm of the Borealis, the Moon and the Stars. As each new day dawns, I will go forth and fulfil my true purpose in life. So mote it be!" Light the candle and let it burn all the way down.

GODDESSES OF TRANSFORMATION

Ariadne

In the deepening twilight she stands just inside her cave beckoning to you,
"Come," she softly calls, *"follow me into the Labyrinth,*
you will not lose your way. Fear not the Minotaur that dwells within the dark hollows."
And like a snake unfolding, you follow her,
venturing forth into the twisting passages that twist and turn without end.
"Do not fear *the darkness within,* for it is the world without that contains the
Minotaur." In the shadows her *essential power gleams* and
serpents entwine around her arms.
In her hand she holds the *thread,* unravelling, unwinding …
"Will you come with me, my sister, will you come?"

Ariadne is the Minoan Goddess of Divination, she is also represented as the Cretan Snake Goddess of Transformation, a female figure in a trance like state, holding serpents in her hands as she dances a hypnotic dance.

In legend, Ariadne was the daughter of King Minos of Crete and the Priestess of the Labyrinth. The Labyrinth at Knossos held a dreadful family secret. King Minos had angered the God Poseidon by keeping a beautiful white bull for himself, instead of giving it in sacrifice to the God. In revenge, Poseidon made the King's wife fall in love with a bull, and from this unnatural union, the monstrous Minotaur was born, half man and half bull. King Minos had a labyrinth built as a prison for the Minotaur. The only person to know how to escape from the labyrinth was its creator, Daedalus, but the king threw him in prison to prevent his revealing the secret. Minos put his daughter, the princess Ariadne, in charge of the labyrinth. He fed the Minotaur upon young Athenians who were sent to him as tribute. One year the hero Theseus arrived from Athens, with the intention of entering the labyrinth and killing the monster. Ariadne fell in love with Theseus and promised to help him in his task, if he would take her back to Athens and marry her. This meant betraying her father and her people so there would be no turning back for Ariadne. She gave Theseus a magical sword and a ball of red wool from a fleece that she had spun. He attached the ball of thread to the door post and played it out behind him as he went. When he found the Minotaur in the innermost part of the Labyrinth, he was able to slay it with the magical sword, and then he was able to make his way back out of the labyrinth by following the thread.

Theseus left for Athens, taking Ariadne with him, however all did not bode well for Ariadne. Theseus did not share the love that Ariadne felt for him and he chose another for his lover instead. He left Ariadne on the island of Naxos, where they had stopped on the way back to Athens. Ariadne was heartbroken, devastated by his betrayal. She remained on Naxos where she was wooed by Dionysus, the God of Wine, and guardian of the island. He married her, she became immortal and he took her wedding diadem and set it in the heavens to her eternal glory, and its jewels turned to stars, to form the constellation Corona Borealis. The brightest star of this is named Alpheta, from 'alpha' and 'eta', the first and last letters of Ariadne's name. This is depicted in the famous painting by Titian, which hangs in the National Gallery, of Dionysus, who is there referred to by his Roman name, Bacchus.

The remarkable fact is that, in Wales, this constellation was said to be the castle of Arianhrod. The similarity of these Goddesses' names may not be a coincidence: long ago they may have been one and the same, as the traditions associating them with the Northern Crown go back thousands of years. Since the Welsh regarded these stars as a place of the dead, probably the Labyrinth was likewise symbolic of the soul's wanderings in the Underworld. Although we are introduced to Ariadne as a mortal princess, Homer described her as being "lovely-haired", a title he normally reserved solely for Goddesses. The symbolism of Ariadne's thread indicates that she, like Hecate, was a guide for the spirit on its journey into the after life. She too was 'of the Labyrinth'.

Two statuettes found in the ruins of the palace of Minos depict bare breasted women with bell skirts holding snakes. They may have represented the Cretan Snake Goddess, or priestesses dressed as their deity. Either way, it is thought that they are also aspects of Ariadne, and that the snake was sacred to her as a symbol of earth, winding its way as if through a maze, and periodically sloughing its own skin, which epitomised the resurrection of the dead.

In addition to being the guardian of the Labyrinth, Ariadne had a special maze-patterned dance floor, also designed by Daedalus, and is said to have instituted a 'dance of the Lady of the

Labyrinth'. This connects her with the mysteries of life, for the maze is symbolic of the many paths in life, and is the path of initiation and also the womb, the female mystery of life and death. Ariadne teaches us to go into ourselves, to look within, to our intuition for guidance. She can help us to look at new possibilities, or to find the solution to a sticky problem, and with ingenuity, to find our way out of difficulties. She can help us make new choices, when those choices may be against what others envisage for us. As a weaving Goddess, she helps us to understand our fate and our purpose. Her symbols are the maze, thread, distaff and spindle, also the golden diadem. Her gems are rubies. Her animals are the bull and the snake and her favourite offerings are wine and honey. Ariadne can also help us to recover from a broken heart, to rise above the pain and betrayal that we might feel and to look beyond, to find love again. As Goddess of Divination, she is an excellent Goddess to work with when developing your psychic and intuitive abilities.

Ariadne Spell to Overcome Fear
By Seldiy Bate

Aim: This spell is helpful when you fear what someone else's reaction might be and therefore become stuck and scared to take action.

Tools: A photo or picture of Ariadne with snakes around her arms, black cloth over a table, as an altar, one black candle, one red candle, one white candle and appropriate holders for them.

What is it that you fear, at this time? Do you fear rejection, or ridicule? These are emotions that link you to a negative emotion and it is Ariadne's domain to help you get to know yourself better. Or do you fear something outside of you, something that you try to avoid? Do you have a phobia of snakes, for instance? For this spell you need a picture of Ariadne with her snakes, as the snake is the symbol of mysteries, of wisdom, healing and beautiful regeneration. You can meditate on the hidden meaning of the picture and this would be one way of completing the spell. If you wish to take it further, then proceed as follows: place the candles in a triangle formation, the white in the centre and behind the other two. The black and red in front, black on the left, red on the right. Place the picture of Ariadne on the altar and, if possible, also have an extra image of a snake, it can be a decorative object, a picture or even a piece of jewellery. If it is jewellery, have it on your altar when you begin the spell.

GODDESSES OF TRANSFORMATION

Create a sacred space as detailed in Chapter One. Make sure you're not going to be disturbed, and spend a little time thinking about transformation and how you intend to call it into being.

When you are ready, imagine yourself in a protective circle and say: "I am protected by this circle! I do not fear the magic of the Goddess, for her protection is around me and her wisdom is within me!"

Light the white candle. Now begin the Ariadne chant, repeat it several times and build it up. Dancing or swaying with it will build up the energy.

"Be you here with me, Ariadne! Face my fear with me, Ariadne!

Weave this charm with me, Ariadne! Cast the harm from me, Ariadne!"

Stop when you feel you have built up the power and take the black candle. Actually hold the candle in both hands (in or out of its holder, whichever is easier). See this candle as the fear and really feel that fear, putting it into the fabric of the candle. You may feel shaky, apprehensive or frightened, but know that no harm will come to you and that your fear will be banished. But you must feel it, in order to get rid of it. Place the candle back in its position and light it. Now hold the red candle. This candle is your defence against the fear, see it as your own courage, your confidence, your way forward. Put it back in its position and light it.

If you have a piece of snake jewellery, put it on now. Look at the picture.

Look at the white candle. It is the light that guides you. Ariadne is walking with you. She and you will face this fear together and she will not leave your side. Really feel the power within yourself and recall it when it is needed. Thank Ariadne in your own way and extinguish the white candle, allow the circle around you to dissolve, knowing that you are protected. Leave the black and red candles to burn down. Light the white candle at any time, especially when you wish to place yourself in Ariadne's wise and courageous light.

Visualisation to Meet Ariadne in the Labyrinth

Aim: To help you to heal your broken heart, to transcend the pain and to find love once again within yourself.

Tools: A photo of statue of Ariadne, pale blue candle, lavender oil, black candle, juniper oil, candlesticks, and frankincense incense.

Purification Bath Instructions
- Draw a warm bath
- Add rock salt and lavender bath salts or 4 drops of essential oil and juniper oil to the water.

Start by taking a purification bath. Rinse your hair with the purifying water so that your aura is completely clear. Prepare your sacred space as detailed in Chapter One. Light the incense. Call upon the Goddess Ariadne, also known as the Cretan Snake Goddess of Transformation:

"I call upon you Ariadne, Goddess of the Snake. Inspire me with your trance so that I can let go of that which I no longer need. Empower me with your serpent energy and help me to shed my old skin and reveal within a new skin, a new me. Ariadne, I bid you, hail and welcome!"

Anoint your pale blue candle with lavender oil and say aloud:

"Great Goddess Ariadne, I ask for help. Heal my emotional pain from my past, mend my broken heart, give me the insight to transcend this emotional heartache to become whole again, to love again. As this healing candle burns, may my wounds be healed once more." Light the candle and say: "So mote it be!"

Close your eyes and imagine yourself at the entrance to a cave. As you enter you see the Goddess Ariadne ahead of you standing before the entrance to a tunnel, from which there glows a mysterious light. She has snakes entwined around her arms and dances, as if in a trance-like state. As you approach her she speaks to you, still gently swaying and dancing with the sensuous rhythm of a snake. What does she say? How do you feel? Tell her about your heartache and emotional pain. Ask for her help in moving forwards. She leads you into the labyrinth, as you follow her down the tunnel, you come to a fork. She stops and asks you to choose which path to take, the left or the right. She tells you that there you will find the answer that you seek. You choose a path and proceed alone, after a while you come to a pool of water set into the side of the rock. You stop to gaze into this pool of darkened water, the flickering light of flaming torches that line the walls reflecting in the water, making it seem alive. Gaze into the pool and see an image form in the water. Gaze upon this for a while. A movement in the water disturbs the image as a water snake rises to the surface and looks at you. What colour is the snake? Are you afraid? You see something in the water and reach in, pulling out a black candle, a symbol with which you shall burn away all that no longer serves you. The snake moves towards you and entwines itself around your wrist, and you find yourself swaying with the rhythm of a drum, a drum that you can hear softly from deep within the labyrinth. The drum becomes louder and seems to be moving towards you. Louder and louder it becomes, until you turn around and find yourself face to face with a giant beast, part man, part bull, with large horns upon his head: you gaze upon the Minotaur. It was not the drums you heard, but the sound of his hooves upon the ground. You sense his power and gaze into his black eyes. All at once, you realise that he represents your fears, and that you have overcome them by facing him here and now. You stare into his eyes, safe in the knowledge that despite his physical strength you are his equal in power. He turns and takes his leave of you, and you return to the crossroads, where the Goddess Ariadne awaits you. She reaches out her hand to you and the snake leaves your arm and entwines itself around hers. She leads you back to the entrance of the labyrinth and you take your leave, thanking Ariadne for her help and wisdom, secure in the knowledge that you can return at any time. She continues her dance, becoming ever deeper in trance and smiles, ever present and yet far away. You emerge from the cave and see your altar before you, with yourself sitting or lying before it and your pale blue healing candle burning brightly. Return back to yourself and start to bring your awareness back into your body. Wiggle your toes and in your own time open your eyes. Take your black candle and anoint it with juniper oil for purification. Say aloud that which you wish to be rid of. End with the affirmation:

"I release all that no longer serves me. As this candle burns, let it be gone from my life."

Remember that this is also good for removing negative attributes from yourself as well as negative things which are in your life. Perhaps it is old emotional and behavioural patterns, old attitudes and negative thinking which also need to be released at this time. Let your candles burn all the way down.

Bibliography

Chapter 2
(i) Adapted from Orphic Hymn to Aphrodite.
(ii) Edited and adapted from *The Gods Within* by Jean Williams and Zachary Cox, Moondust Books, 2008.
(iii) Poem by Sappho, 6th Century BC poet.
(iv) Hymn of the Seven Hathors from the Temple of Dendera.
(v) Inscription from the temple of Sais, Egypt.
(vi) Inscription from the temple on the island of Ios.
(vii) A prayer from the 14th Century BC.

Chapter 3
(i) Hymn to Hecate – The Orphic Hymns (1st - 3rd C. AD) from *The Goddess Hekate*, edited by Stephen Ronan.
(ii) References from K.F. Smith, Hekate's Suppers; from *The Goddess Hekate*, edited by Stephen Ronan.
(iii) Adapted from *The Witches' Goddess* by Janet and Stewart Farrar, Hale Publications, 1987.

Chapter 4
(i) Adapted from *The Gods Within*, by Jean Williams and Zachary Cox, Moondust Books, 2008.
(ii) Adapted from *The Goddess Speaks*, Dee Poth, Sibyl Publications, 1998.
(iii) Adapted from the Orphic Hymn to Nike.
(iv) Homeric Hymn to Victory.
(v) Adapted from the Orphic Hymn to Tyche

About the Authors

Carrie Kirkpatrick is a television producer, photographer, and author. She runs Divine Media (www.divinemedia.tv), producing television programmes about the esoteric world and historical mysteries and is a prolific photographer.

Carrie runs Goddess Enchantment workshops which have inspired the creation of these workbooks. Many of the images in these books were taken during the workshops, illustrating a visual and sensory celebration in honour of the Goddesses.

The images in the *Goddess Enchantment, Magic & Spells* books have been developed into the *Goddess Enchantment Oracle App*. For more information about Goddess Enchantment workshops visit www.carriekirkpatrick.com.

Markus Wolfson was a writer who has had published many articles on esoteric subjects, short stories and a novel under various pen names. He was an ordained priest of Fortuna, a Goddess he first became aware of when he was nine or ten. From that age too, he was fascinated by esoteric subjects and disciplines and put this down to having Neptune in his twelfth house. As a priest of Fortuna, he tried to show people how she can guide them and give them abundance and good luck. Markus Wolfson sadly passed away in 2015.

Seldiy Bate is a musician and a mystic. She was initiated into Wicca many Moons ago and has taught and written about spellcraft and magick. She has spent many years researching the divine impulse behind folk customs and music and is inspired in everything she does, by the Muses, the many forms of the Goddess.

Also Available from Author Carrie Kirkpatrick

Goddess Enchantment, Magic and Spells takes you on a journey into the realms of magic and legend, as we retrace the myths of the Goddesses of old with a fresh perspective that makes them accessible in the 21st Century. Carrie Kirkpatrick opens the doorway to the magical realms of the Goddesses, inviting you to partake in visualizations, spells and rituals designed to help you fulfill your potential. See the Goddesses come to life in vibrant and magical photographs, connect to them and gain from their inspirational blessings.

Goddesses of the Seasons takes you through the Wheel Of The Year, incorporating both traditional and fresh new ways to celebrate the Fire Festivals, the Equinoxes and the Solstices. Visit www.carriekirkpatrick.com for more information about this title.